The Right of Nations to Self-Determination

Selected Writings
BY V. I. LENIN

GREENWOOD PRESS, PUBLISHERS
WESTPORT, CONNECTICUT

Library of Congress Cataloging in Publication Data

Lenin, Vladimir Il'ich, 1870-1924.
  The right of nations to self-determination.

    Translation of O prave natsii na samoopredelenie.
    Reprint of the ed. published by International Pub-
  lishers, New York.
    Includes bibliographical references.
    1. Self-determination, National. 2. Minorities-
  Russia. I. Title.
  [JX4054.I42 1977]   323.1   77-22314
  ISBN 0-8371-9731-7

320.157
L566

Originally published in 1951 by International Publishers Co., Inc.,
New York

Reprinted with the permission of International Publishers Co., Inc.

Reprinted in 1977 by Greenwood Press, Inc.

Library of Congress catalog card number 77-22314

ISBN 0-8371-9731-7

Printed in the United States of America

EDITOR'S NOTE

Several of Lenin's basic theoretical essays on the national question are brought together in this volume. They analyze the national question specifically and historically in Russia, Norway, Poland, and Ireland and discuss national oppression, colonialism, social chauvinism, and opportunism in the national question. The book underlines the relationship of the national question to imperialism and shows how the struggle for democracy and national liberation is integrated with the fight for socialism.

In these essays, Lenin exposes various errors in dealing with the national question. He points out the concrete tasks of the working class within both the oppressed and oppressing nations in the struggle for self-determination.

In view of the key importance of the national question in the world today, this collection is particularly valuable. *The Right of Nations to Self-Determination* forms a companion volume with Joseph Stalin's *Marxism and the National Question,* which was written at about the same time and which Lenin regarded as a masterful contribution to Marxism.

CONTENTS

The Right of Nations

to Self-Determination

Point 9 of the program of the Russian Marxists, which deals with the right of nations to self-determination, has given rise lately (as we have already pointed out in *Prosveshcheniye**) to a regular crusade of the opportunists. The Russian Liquidator† Semkovsky in the St. Petersburg Liquidationist newspaper, the Bundist‡ Liebman and the Ukrainian Social-Nationalist Yurkevich in their respective journals, severely came down upon this point and treated it with an air of supreme contempt. There is no doubt that this "twelve language invasion" of opportunism into our Marxist program is closely connected with present-day nationalistic vacillations in general. Hence, we think that a detailed analysis of this question is opportune. We shall only observe that none of the above-mentioned opportunists has adduced a single independent argument; all of them merely repeat what was said by Rosa Luxem-

* *Prosveshcheniye (Enlightenment)*, a Bolshevik monthly journal, published in St. Petersburg, Russia, in 1911-14.—*Ed.*

† Liquidators, name applied during the reaction following the defeat of the Russian Revolution of 1905 to the Mensheviks, who were out to destroy, *i.e.*, liquidate, the illegal, revolutionary party of the proletariat and to obtain, at the cost of renouncing its program and tactics, the right to exist as a legal, "open" workers' party. On the national question the Liquidators supported the Bundists' slogan of "national-cultural autonomy."—*Ed.*

‡ The Bund was the abbreviated name for the "General Jewish Workers' Alliance in Lithuania, Poland and Russia" (founded in 1897); it pursued a national line which reflected the petty-bourgeois tendencies in the working-class movement. The Bund demanded that the party be organized along federative principles—by nationalities—and that it, the Bund, be the sole representative of the Jewish proletariat. In 1905 it put forward the demand for so-called "cultural-national autonomy," which Lenin characterized as a nationalist, bourgeois, reactionary demand that would lead to the isolation of the proletarians of the various nationalities. Lenin, Stalin, and the Bolshevik Party fought mercilessly against the nationalism of the Bund.—*Ed.*

burg* in her long Polish article of 1908-09, "The National Question and Autonomy." In our exposition we shall deal mainly with the "original" arguments of this last-named author.

WHAT IS SELF-DETERMINATION OF NATIONS?

Naturally, this is the first question to arise when any attempt is made to consider what self-determination is, from a Marxist viewpoint. What is meant by that term? Should we seek for an answer in legal definitions deduced from all sorts of "general concepts" of law? Or should we seek an answer in the historical and economic study of the national movements?

It is not surprising that the Semkovskys, Liebmans, and Yurkeviches did not even think of raising this question, but limited themselves merely to sneering about the "obscurity" of the Marxist program, apparently not knowing in their simplicity that self-determination of nations is dealt with not only in the Russian program of 1903, but also in the resolution of the London International Congress of 1896 (with which I shall deal in detail in the proper place). What is surprising is the fact that Rosa Luxemburg, who declaims a great deal about the alleged abstract and metaphysical nature of the point in question should herself succumb to the sin of abstraction and metaphysics. It is Rosa Luxemburg herself who is continually straying into generalities about self-determination (including the very amusing speculation on the question of how the will of the nation is to be ascertained), without anywhere clearly and precisely asking herself whether the issue is determined by juridical definitions or by the experience of the national movements throughout the world.

A precise formulation of this question, which a Marxist cannot avoid, would at once have shaken nine-tenths of Rosa Luxemburg's arguments. This is not the first time national movements have arisen in Russia, nor are they peculiar to Russia alone. Throughout the world, the period of the final victory of capitalism over feudalism has been linked with national movements. The economic basis of these movements is the fact that in order to achieve complete

---

* Rosa Luxemburg (1871-1919), prominent figure in the Polish and German Social-Democratic movement, one of the founders of the Communist Party of Germany, a passionate revolutionary and tireless champion of the cause of the working class. Lenin had a high opinion of her, but at the same time sharply criticized her semi-Menshevik position on a number of important questions of revolutionary Marxism, particularly the national question.—*Ed.*

victory for commodity production the bourgeoisie must capture the home market, must have politically united territories with a population speaking the same language, and all obstacles to the development of this language and to its consolidation in literature must be removed. Language is the most important means of human intercourse. Unity of language and its unimpeded development are most important conditions for genuinely free and extensive commercial intercourse on a scale commensurate with modern capitalism, for a free and broad grouping of the population in all its separate classes and, lastly, for the establishment of close connection between the market and each and every proprietor, big or little, seller and buyer.

Therefore, the tendency of every national movement is towards the formation of *national states*, under which these requirements of modern capitalism are best satisfied. The profoundest economic factors drive towards this goal, and therefore, for the whole of Western Europe, nay, for the entire civilized world, the *typical, normal* state for the capitalist period is the national state.

Consequently, if we want to learn the meaning of self-determination of nations not by juggling with legal definitions, or "inventing" abstract definitions, but by examining the historical and economic conditions of the national movements, we shall inevitably reach the conclusion that self-determination of nations means the political separation of these nations from alien national bodies, the formation of an independent national state.

Later on we shall see still other reasons why it would be incorrect to understand the right to self-determination to mean anything but the right to separate state existence. At present, we must deal with Rosa Luxemburg's efforts to "dismiss" the unavoidable conclusion that the striving to form a national state rests on deep economic foundations.

Rosa Luxemburg is quite familiar with Kautsky's pamphlet *Nationality and Internationality*. (Supplement to *Die Neue Zeit*, No. 1, 1907-08; Russian translation in the magazine *Nauchnaya Mysl* [*Scientific Thought*], Riga, 1910.) She knows that Kautsky, after carefully analyzing the question of the national state in Chapter Four of that pamphlet, arrived at the conclusion that Otto Bauer "*underestimates* the force of the urge to create a national state" (p. 23). Rosa Luxemburg herself quotes the following words of Kautsky: "The national state is the form of state that is *most suitable* for present-day conditions" (*i.e.,* capitalist, civilized, eco-

11

nomically progressive conditions, as distinguished from medieval, pre-capitalist, etc.), "it is the form in which it can best fulfill its tasks" (that is, the task of securing the freest, widest, and speediest development of capitalism). We must add to this a still more precise concluding remark by Kautsky: heterogeneous nation states (what are called nationality states as distinguished from national states) are "always states whose internal constitution has for some reason or other remained abnormal or underdeveloped" (backward). Needless to say, Kautsky speaks of abnormality exclusively in the sense of lack of conformity with what is best adapted to the requirements of developing capitalism.

The question now is, how did Rosa Luxemburg treat Kautsky's historical-economic conclusions on this point? Are they right or wrong? Is Kautsky right in his historical-economic theory, or is Bauer, whose theory has a psychological basis? What is the connection between Bauer's undoubted "national opportunism," his defense of cultural-national autonomy, his nationalistic infatuation ("here and there an emphasis on the national aspect," as Kautsky put it), his "enormous exaggeration of the national aspect and complete oblivion to the international aspect" (Kautsky)—and his underestimation of the force of the urge to create a national state?

Rosa Luxemburg did not even raise this question. She failed to notice this connection. She did not weigh the *totality* of Bauer's theoretical views. She did not even draw a contrast between the historical-economic and the psychological theory of the national question. She confined herself to the following remarks in criticism of Kautsky: "This 'best' national state is only an abstraction which can easily be developed and defended theoretically, but which does not correspond to reality." (*Przeglad Socjal-Demokratyczny [Social-Democratic Review]*, 1908, No. 6, p. 499.)*

And in corroboration of this bold statement there follow arguments to the effect that the "right to self-determination" of small nations is rendered illusory by the development of the great capitalist powers and by imperialism.

"Can one seriously speak," exclaims Rosa Luxemburg, "about the 'self-determination' of the formally independent Montenegrins, Bulgarians, Rumanians, Serbs, Greeks, partly even the Swiss, whose independence is itself a result of the political struggle and the diplomatic game of the 'Concert of Europe'?" (p. 500.)

* Theoretical organ of the Social-Democrats of Poland and Lithuania, published in Cracow 1902-1910.—*Ed.*

The state that best suits the conditions is "not a national state, as Kautsky believes, but a predatory state." Several score of figures are quoted relating to the size of British, French, and other colonies.

Reading such arguments one cannot help marvelling how the author contrived not to understand *what's what!* To teach Kautsky with a serious mien that small states are economically dependent on big ones, that a struggle is going on between the bourgeois states for the predatory suppression of other nations, that imperialism and colonies exist—savors of ridiculously childish attempts to be clever, for all this is altogether irrelevant to the subject. Not only small states, but even Russia, for example, is economically entirely dependent on the power of the imperialist finance capital of the "rich" bourgeois countries. Not only the miniature Balkan states, but even America in the nineteenth century was economically a colony of Europe, as Marx pointed out in *Capital*.[1] Kautsky, and every Marxist, is well aware of this, of course, but it has nothing whatever to do with the question of national movements and the national state.

For the question of the political self-determination of nations in bourgeois society, and of their independence as states, Rosa Luxemburg has substituted the question of their economic independence. This is as intelligent as if someone, in discussing the demand in the program for the supremacy of parliament, *i.e.,* the assembly of people's representatives, in a bourgeois state, were to expound the perfectly correct conviction that big capital is supreme under any regime in a bourgeois country.

There is no doubt that the greater part of Asia, the most populous part of the world, consists either of colonies of the "Great Powers" or of states which are extremely dependent and oppressed as nations. But does this commonly known circumstance in any way shake the undoubted fact that in Asia itself the conditions for the most complete development of commodity production, for the freest, widest, and speediest growth of capitalism, have been created only in Japan, *i.e.,* only in an independent national state? This state is a bourgeois state, therefore, it, itself, has begun to oppress other nations and to enslave colonies. We cannot say whether Asia will have time before the downfall of capitalism to become crystallized into a system of independent national states, like Europe; but it remains an undisputed fact that capitalism, having awakened Asia, has called forth national movements everywhere in that continent, too; that the tendency of these movements is towards the creation of national states there; that the best conditions for the development of capitalism are ensured precisely by such states. The example of Asia speaks in *favor* of Kautsky and *against* Rosa Luxemburg.

The example of the Balkan states also speaks against her, for everyone can see now that the best conditions for the development of capitalism in the Balkans are created precisely in proportion to the creation of independent national states in that peninsula.

Therefore, Rosa Luxemburg notwithstanding, the example of the whole of progressive, civilized mankind, the example of the Balkans and the example of Asia prove that Kautsky's proposition is absolutely correct: the national state is the rule and the "norm" of capitalism; the heterogeneous nation state represents backwardness, or is an exception. From the standpoint of national relations, the best conditions for the development of capitalism are undoubtedly provided by the national state. This does not mean, of course, that such a state, based on bourgeois relations, could eliminate the exploitation and oppression of nations. It only means that Marxists cannot ignore the powerful *economic* factors that give rise to the aspiration to create national states. It means that "self-determination of nations" in the program of the Marxists *cannot,* from a historical-economic point of view, have any other meaning than political self-determination, political independence, the formation of a national state.

On what conditions the bourgeois-democratic demand for a "national state" is to be supported from a Marxist, *i.e.,* class proletarian, point of view will be dealt with in detail later on. At present we confine ourselves to the definition of the *concept* "self-determination" and must only note that Rosa Luxemburg *knows* what this concept means ("national state"), whereas her opportunist partisans, the Liebmans, the Semkovskys, the Yurkeviches *do not even know that!*

THE HISTORICALLY CONCRETE PRESENTATION
OF THE QUESTION

The categorical demand of Marxist theory in examining any social question is that the question be formulated within *definite* historical limits, and if it refers to a particular country (*e.g.,* the national program for a given country), the specific features that distinguish that country from others within the same historical epoch be taken into account.

What does this categorical demand of Marxism imply as regards the question we are discussing?

First of all, it implies that a strict distinction must be drawn between two periods of capitalism, which differ radically from each other as far as the national movement is concerned. On the one hand, the period of the downfall of feudalism and absolutism, the period of the formation of bourgeois-democratic society and state, when the national movements for the first time become mass movements and in one way or another draw *all* classes of the population into politics by means of the press, participation in representative institutions, etc. On the other hand, we have the period of definitely crystallized capitalist states with a long-established constitutional regime, with a strongly developed antagonism between the proletariat and the bourgeoisie—the period that may be called the eve of the downfall of capitalism.

The typical features of the first period are the awakening of national movements and the drawing of the peasants, the most numerous and the most "sluggish" section of the population, into these movements, in connection with the struggle for political liberty in general and for national rights in particular. The typical features of the second period are the absence of mass bourgeois-democratic movements; the fact that developed capitalism, while bringing the nations that have already been fully drawn into commercial intercourse closer together and causing them to intermingle to an increasing degree, pushes into the forefront the antagonism between internationally united capital and the international labor movement.

Of course, the two periods cannot be separated into watertight compartments; they are connected by numerous transitional links, while the various countries differ from each other in the rapidity of their national development, in national composition and distribution of their population, and so forth. The Marxists of a given country cannot proceed to draw up their national program without taking into account all these general historical and concrete state conditions.

And it is just here that we come up against the weakest point in the arguments of Rosa Luxemburg. With extraordinary zeal she embellishes her article with a collection of "strong" words against point 9 of our program, declaring it to be "sweeping," "a platitude," "a metaphysical phrase," and so on *ad infinitum*. It would be

15

natural to expect that an author who so magnificently condemns metaphysics (in the Marxist sense, *i.e.,* anti-dialectics) and empty abstractions would set us an example of how to make a concrete historical analysis of the question. We are discussing the national program of the Marxists of a definite country, Russia, in a definite period, the beginning of the twentieth century. But does Rosa Luxemburg raise the question as to *what historical* period Russia is passing through, as to *what are the concrete* specific features of the national question and the national movements of that *particular* country in that *particular* period?

No! She says absolutely nothing about it! In her work you will not find even the hint of an analysis of how the national question stands in *Russia* in the present historical period, or of the specific features of *Russia* in this particular respect!

We are told that the national question stands differently in the Balkans than in Ireland; that Marx appraised the Polish and Czech national movements in the concrete conditions of 1848 in this way (a page of excerpts from Marx); that Engels appraised the struggle of the forest cantons of Switzerland against Austria and the battle of Morgarten which took place in 1315 in that way (a page of quotations from Engels with Kautsky's commentaries on them); that Lassalle regarded the peasant war in Germany of the sixteenth century as reactionary, etc.

It cannot be said that these remarks and quotations are remarkable for their novelty, but, at all events, it is interesting for the reader to recall again and again precisely how Marx, Engels, and Lassalle approached the analysis of concrete historical questions in individual countries. And a perusal of these instructive quotations from Marx and Engels reveals most strikingly the ridiculous position Rosa Luxemburg has placed herself in. Eloquently and angrily she preaches the need for a concrete historical analysis of the national question in various countries at various periods; but she makes not the *slightest* attempt to determine through *what* historical stage in the development of capitalism *Russia* is passing at the beginning of the twentieth century or the *specific features* of the national question in this country. Rosa Luxemburg gives examples of how *others* have treated the question in a Marxist fashion, as if deliberately stressing how often good intentions pave the road to hell, how often good counsels cover up unwillingness or inability to follow these counsels in practice.

Here is one of her edifying comparisons. In protesting against

16

the demand for the independence of Poland, Rosa Luxemburg refers to her work of 1898, in which she demonstrated the rapid "industrial development of Poland" and the sale of the latter's manufactured goods in Russia. Needless to say, no conclusion whatever can be drawn from this on the question of the *right* of self-determination; it only proves the disappearance of the old, squire-ridden Poland, etc. But Rosa Luxemburg always imperceptibly passes on to the conclusion that among the factors that unite Russia and Poland, the purely economic factors of modern capitalist relations now predominate.

Then our Rosa passes on to the question of autonomy, and though her article is entitled "The National Question and Autonomy," *in general,* she begins to argue that the Kingdom of Poland has an *exclusive* right to autonomy (*cf. Prosveshcheniye,* 1913, No. 12). In order to support the right of Poland to autonomy, Rosa Luxemburg evidently judges the state system of Russia by its economic and political and sociological characteristics and everyday life —a totality of traits, which produce the concept "Asiatic despotism." (*Przeglad,* No. 12, p. 137.)

It is common knowledge that a state system of that type possesses great stability in those cases where completely patriarchal pre-capitalist traits are predominant in the economic system and where commodity production and class differentiation are hardly developed. If, however, in a country where the state system bears a very distinct *pre-*capitalist character, there is a nationally delimited region where capitalism is *rapidly* developing, then the more rapidly that capitalism develops, the greater will be the antagonism between it and the *pre-*capitalist state system, and the more probably will the more progressive region separate from the whole—with which it is connected not by "modern capitalistic," but by "Asiatic-despotic" ties.

Thus, Rosa Luxemburg's reasoning is faulty even on the question of the social structure of the government in Russia in relation to bourgeois Poland; and she does not even raise the question of the concrete, historical, specific features of the national movements in Russia.

This question we must deal with.

CONCRETE SPECIFIC FEATURES OF THE NATIONAL QUESTION IN RUSSIA AND RUSSIA'S BOURGEOIS-DEMOCRATIC REFORMATION

"In spite of the elasticity of the principle of 'the right of nations to self-determination,' which is a mere platitude, being, obviously, equally applicable not only to the nations inhabiting Russia, but also to the nations inhabiting Germany and Austria, Switzerland and Sweden, America, and Australia, we do not find it in the programs of any of the present-day Socialist parties. . . ." (*Przeglad*, No. 6, p. 483.)

This is what Rosa Luxemburg writes at the very beginning of her crusade against point 9 of the Marxists' program. In trying to foist on us the conception of this point in the program as a "mere platitude" Rose Luxemburg herself falls victim to this error, alleging with amusing audacity that this point is "obviously, equally applicable" to Russia, Germany, etc.

Obviously, we reply, Rosa Luxemburg decided to make her article a collection of errors in logic suitable for schoolboy exercises. For Rosa Luxemburg's tirade is absolute nonsense and a mockery of the historically concrete presentation of the question.

Interpreting the Marxist program in a Marxist and not in a childish way, it is very easy to surmise that it refers to bourgeois-democratic national movements. If that is the case, and it undoubtedly is the case, it is "obvious" that this program "sweepingly," as a "platitude," etc., refers to *all* instances of bourgeois-democratic national movements. And had Rosa Luxemburg given the slightest thought to this, she would have come to the no less obvious conclusion that our program refers *only* to cases where such a movement is actually in existence.

Had she pondered over these obvious considerations, Rosa Luxemburg would have easily perceived what nonsense she was uttering. In accusing *us* of uttering a "platitude" she uses *against us* the argument that no mention is made of the right to self-determination in the programs of those countries where there are *no* bourgeois-democratic national movements! A remarkably clever argument!

A comparison of the political and economic development of various countries as well as of the Marxist programs is of enormous importance from the standpoint of Marxism, for there can be no doubt that all modern states are of the same capitalist nature and are subject to the same law of development. But such a comparison must be drawn in a sensible way. The elementary condition required for this is the elucidation of the question of whether the historical periods of the development of the countries compared are at all *comparable*. For instance, only absolute ignoramuses (such as Prince E. Trubetskoy* in *Russkaya Mysl†*) are capable of "comparing" the agrarian program of the Russian Marxists with those of Western Europe, for our program answers the question regarding a *bourgeois-democratic* agrarian reformation, whereas in the Western countries no such question exists.

The same applies to the national question. In most Western countries this question was settled long ago. It is ridiculous to seek in the programs of Western Europe for an answer to non-existent questions. Rosa Luxemburg has lost sight of the most important thing here, *viz.,* the difference between countries where the bourgeois-democratic reformation has long been completed and those where it has not yet been completed. This difference is the crux of the matter. Her complete disregard of this difference transforms Rosa Luxemburg's exceedingly long article into a collection of empty, meaningless platitudes.

In Western, continental Europe, the period of the bourgeois-democratic revolutions embraces a fairly definite portion of time, approximately from 1789 to 1871. This was precisely the period of national movements and the creation of national states. When this period drew to a close Western Europe had been transformed into a settled system of bourgeois states, which, as a general rule, were national uniform states. Therefore, to seek the right of self-determination in the programs of present-day West-European Socialists is to betray one's ignorance of the ABC of Marxism.

In Eastern Europe and in Asia the period of bourgeois-democratic revolutions only began in 1905. The revolutions in Russia, Persia, Turkey, and China, the wars in the Balkans, such is the chain of world events of *our* period in our "Orient." And only the blind can fail to see in this chain of events the awakening of a *whole series* of bourgeois-democratic national movements, strivings to create nationally independent and nationally uniform states. It is precisely and solely because Russia and the neighboring countries are passing through this period that we require an item in our program on the right of nations to self-determination.

*E. Trubetskoy (1863-1919), an ideologist of Russian imperialism, a member of the bourgeois-liberal Constitutional-Democratic Party (Cadets).—*Ed.*

†*Russkaya Mysl* (*Russian Thought*), a liberal Populist monthly, first appeared in St. Petersburg in 1880.—*Ed.*

But let us continue the quotation from Rosa Luxemburg's article a little further. She writes:

"In particular, the program of a party which is operating in a state with an extremely mixed national composition and for which the national question is a matter of first-rate importance—the program of the Austrian Social-Democratic Party—does not contain the principle of the right of nations to self-determination." (*Ibid.*)

Thus, an attempt is made to convince the reader by the example of Austria "in particular." Let us see whether this example is a reasonable one by examining this definite historical case.

In the first place, we raise the fundamental question of the completion of the bourgeois-democratic revolution. In Austria this revolution began in 1848, and was over in 1867. Since then, for nearly half a century, there has prevailed what on the whole is an established bourgeois constitution on the basis of which a legal workers' party is legally functioning.

Therefore, in the inherent conditions of the development of Austria (*i.e.,* from the standpoint of the development of capitalism in Austria in general, and among its separate nations in particular), there are *no* factors that produce leaps, one of the concomitants of which may be the formation of nationally independent states. In assuming by her comparison that Russia is in an analogous position in this respect, Rosa Luxemburg not only makes a radically wrong, anti-historical assumption, but she involuntarily slips into Liquidationism.

Secondly, the entirely different relations between the nationalities in Austria and in Russia are particularly important for the question we are concerned with. Not only was Austria for a long time a state in which the Germans were predominant, but the Austrian Germans laid claim to hegemony in the German nation as a whole. This "claim," as Rosa Luxemburg (who is seemingly so averse to commonplaces, platitudes, abstractions . . .) will perhaps be kind enough to remember, was defeated in the war of 1866. The German nation predominating in Austria found itself *outside the pale* of the independent German state which finally took shape in 1871. On the other hand, the attempt of the Hungarians to create an independent national state collapsed as far back as 1849, under the blows of the Russian army of serfs.

A very peculiar situation was thus created: a striving on the part of the Hungarians and then of the Czechs, not for separation from Austria, but, on the contrary, for the preservation of Austria's integrity, precisely in order to preserve national independence, which might have been completely crushed by more rapacious and powerful neighbors! Owing to this peculiar situation, Austria assumed the form of a double-centred (dual) state, and is now being transformed into a three-centred (triune) state (Germans, Hungarians, Slavs).

Is there anything like this in Russia? Is there in our country a striving of "alien races" for unity with the Great Russians in order to escape a *worse* national oppression?

It suffices to put this question to see that the comparison between Russia and Austria in the question of self-determination of nations is senseless, platitudinous, and ignorant.

The peculiar conditions in Russia as regards the national question are just the reverse of those we see in Austria. Russia is a state with a single national center—Great Russia. The Great Russians occupy a vast, uninterrupted stretch of territory, and number about 70,000,-000. The specific features of this national state are, first, that "alien races" (which, on the whole, form the majority of the entire population—57 per cent) inhabit the border regions. Second, the oppression of these alien races is much worse than in the neighboring states (and not in the European states alone). Third, in a number of cases the oppressed nationalities inhabiting the border regions have compatriots across the border who enjoy greater national independence (suffice it to mention the Finns, the Swedes, the Poles, the Ukrainians, and the Rumanians along the western and southern frontiers of the state). Fourth, the development of capitalism and the general level of culture are often higher in the border regions inhabited by "alien races" than in the center. Lastly, it is precisely in the neighboring Asian states that we observe incipient bourgeois revolutions and national movements, which partly affect the kindred nationalities within the borders of Russia.

Thus, it is precisely the concrete, historical specific features of the national question in Russia that make the recognition of the right of nations to self-determination in the present period a matter of special urgency in our country.

Incidentally, even from the purely factual aspect, Rosa Luxemburg's assertion that the program of the Austrian Social-Democrats does not contain the recognition of the right of nations to self-determination is incorrect. We need only open the minutes of the Brunn Congress, which adopted the national program, to find the statements by the Ruthenian Social-Democrat Hankevicz on behalf of the entire Ukrainian (Ruthenian) delegation (p. 85 of the minutes), and by the Polish Social-Democrat Reger on behalf of the

21

entire Polish delegation (p. 108), to the effect that one of the aims of the Austrian Social-Democrats of both the above-mentioned nations is to secure national unity, the freedom and independence of their nations. Hence, Austrian Social-Democracy, while not including the right of nations to self-determination directly in its program, nevertheless allows the demand for national independence to be advanced by *sections* of the party. In reality this means, of course, the recognition of the right of nations to self-determination! Thus, Rosa Luxemburg's reference to Austria speaks *against* Rosa Luxemburg in *all* respects.

"PRACTICALNESS" IN THE NATIONAL QUESTION

The opportunists were particularly keen in taking up Rosa Luxemburg's argument that there is nothing "practical" in point 9 of our program. Rosa Luxemburg is so delighted with this argument that in some parts of her article this "slogan" is repeated eight times on a single page.

She writes: Point 9 "gives no practical lead on the day-to-day policy of the proletariat, no practical solution of national problems."

Let us examine this argument, which elsewhere is also formulated in a way that implies that point 9 is either meaningless, or else pledges us to support all national aspirations.

What does the demand for "practicalness" in the national question imply? Either support for all national aspirations; or the answer "yes" or "no" to the question of secession in the case of every nation; or that national demands are immediately "practicable" in general.

Let us consider all these three possible meanings of the demand for "practicalness."

The bourgeoisie, which naturally exercises hegemony (leadership) in the beginning of every national movement, considers it practical to support all national aspirations. But the policy of the proletariat in the national question (as in other questions) supports the bourgeoisie only in a definite direction; it never coincides with the policy of the bourgeoisie. The working class supports the bourgeoisie only in order to secure national peace (which the bourgeoisie cannot bring about completely, which can be achieved only with *complete* democracy) in order to secure equal rights and to create better conditions for the class struggle. Therefore, *against the practicalness* of the bourgeoisie the proletarians advance their *principles* in the national question; they always give the bourgeoisie *only conditional* support. In national affairs the bourgeoisie always strives for privileges or exceptional advantages for its *own* nation; and this is called being "practical." The proletariat is opposed to all privileges, to all exceptionalism. Those who demand that it should be "practical" are trailing in the wake of the bourgeoisie, are falling into opportunism.

The demand for an answer "yes" or "no" to the question of secession in the case of every nation seems to be a very "practical" one. In reality it is absurd; it is metaphysical in theory, and in practice it means subordinating the proletariat to the policy of the bourgeoisie. The bourgeoisie always places its national demands in the forefront. It advances them categorically. For the proletariat, however, these demands are subordinate to the interests of the class struggle. Theoretically, it is impossible to vouch beforehand whether the secession of a given nation from, or its equality with, another nation will complete the bourgeois-democratic revolution; *in either case,* the important thing for the proletariat is to ensure the development of its class. For the bourgeoisie it is important to hamper this development and to put the aims of "its" nation before the aims of the proletariat. That is why the proletariat confines itself, so to say, to the negative demand for the recognition of the *right* to self-determination, without guaranteeing anything to any nation, without undertaking to give *anything at the expense* of another nation.

This may not be "practical," but in reality it is the best guarantee for the achievement of the most democratic of all possible solutions. The proletariat needs *only* these guarantees, whereas the bourgeoisie of every nation requires guarantees for its *own* interests, irrespective of the position of (or the possible disadvantages to) other nations.

The bourgeoisie is most interested in the "practicability" of the given demand—hence the perennial policy of coming to terms with the bourgeoisie of other nations to the detriment of the proletariat. For the proletariat, however, the important thing is to strengthen its class against the bourgeoisie and to educate the masses in the spirit of consistent democracy and socialism.

The opportunists may think this is not "practical," but it is the only real guarantee of a maximum of national equality and peace, in spite of the feudal landlords and the *nationalist* bourgeoisie.

The whole task of the proletarians in the national question is "impractical" from the standpoint of the *nationalist* bourgeoisie of every nation, because, being opposed to all nationalism, the proletarians demand "abstract" equality, they demand that on principle, there shall be no privileges, however slight. Failing to grasp this,

Rosa Luxemburg, by her unwise eulogy of practicalness, opened the gate wide for the opportunists, and especially for opportunist concessions to Great-Russian nationalism.

Why Great-Russian? Because the Great Russians in Russia are an oppressing nation, and opportunism on the national question will naturally be differently expressed among the oppressed nations than among the oppressing nations.

The bourgeoisie of the oppressed nations will call upon the proletariat to support its aspirations unconditionally on the plea that its demands are "practical." It would be more practical to say a plain "yes" in favor of the secession of a *particular* nation than in favor of all nations having the *right* to secede.

The proletariat is opposed to such practicalness. While recognizing equality and an equal right to a national state, it attaches supreme value to the alliance of the proletarians of all nations, and evaluates every national demand, every national separation, *from the angle* of the class struggle of the workers. This call for practicalness is merely a call for the uncritical acceptance of bourgeois aspirations.

We are told: by supporting the right to secession you are supporting the bourgeois nationalism of the oppressed nations. This is what Rosa Luxemburg says, and it is echoed by Semkovsky, the opportunist, who, by the way, is the only representative of Liquidationist ideas on this question in the Liquidationist Newspaper!

Our reply to this is: No, a "practical" solution of this question is important for the bourgeoisie. The important thing for the workers is to distinguish the *principles* of two trends. *If* the bourgeoisie of the oppressed nation fights against the oppressing one, we are always, in every case, and more resolutely than anyone else, *in favor;* for we are the staunchest and the most consistent enemies of oppression. But if the bourgeoisie of the oppressed nation stands for *its own* bourgeois nationalism we are opposed. We fight against the privileges and violence of the oppressing nation, but we do not condone the strivings for privileges on the part of the oppressed nation.

If we do not raise and advocate the slogan of the *right* to secession we shall play into the hands, not only of the bourgeoisie, but also of the feudal landlords and the despotism of the *oppressing* nation. Kautsky long ago advanced this argument against Rosa Luxemburg, and the argument is indisputable. When Rosa Luxemburg, in her anxiety not to "assist" the nationalistic bourgeoisie of Poland, rejects the *right* to secession in the program of the *Russian* Marxists, she is *in fact* assisting the Great-Russian Black-Hundreds.* She is in fact assisting opportunist resignation to the privileges (and worse than privileges) of the Great Russians.

Carried away by the struggle against nationalism in Poland, Rosa Luxemburg has forgotten the nationalism of the Great Russians, although *this* nationalism is the most formidable at the present time, it is the nationalism that is less bourgeois and more feudal, and it is the principal obstacle to democracy and to the proletarian struggle. The bourgeois nationalism of *every* oppressed nation has a general democratic content which is directed *against* oppression, and it is this content that we support *unconditionally,* while strictly distinguishing it from the tendency towards national exceptionalism, while fighting against the tendency of the Polish bourgeoisie to oppress the Jews, etc., etc.

This is "impractical" from the standpoint of a bourgeois and a philistine; but it is the only policy in the national question that is practical, that is based on principles, and that really furthers democracy, liberty, and proletarian unity.

The recognition of the right to secession for all; the appraisal of each concrete question of secession from the point of view of removing all inequality, all privileges, all exceptionalism.

Let us examine the position of an oppressing nation. Can a nation be free if it oppresses other nations? It cannot. The interests of the freedom of the Great-Russian population† demand a struggle against such oppression. The long, age-long history of the suppression of the movements of the oppressed nations, the systematic propaganda in favor of such suppression on the part of the "upper" classes, have created enormous obstacles to the cause of freedom of the Great-Russian people itself, in the form of prejudices, etc.

The Great-Russian Black-Hundreds deliberately foster and fan these prejudices. The Great-Russian bourgeoisie tolerates them or panders to them. The Great-Russian proletariat cannot achieve *its own* aims, cannot clear the road to freedom for itself unless it systematically combats these prejudices.

In Russia, the creation of an independent national state so far

*Tsarist-inspired organizations of ultra-reactionary groups which were responsible for pogroms and other excesses against the revolutionary and even liberal movements.—*Ed.*

† This word appears un-Marxist to a certain L. Vl. in Paris. This L. Vl. is amusingly *"superklug"* (over-clever). This "over-clever" L. Vl. apparently proposes to write an essay on the deletion from our minimum program (having in mind the class struggle!) of the words "population," "people," etc.

remains the privilege of one nation, the Great-Russian nation. We, the Great-Russian proletarians, defend no privileges, and we do not defend this privilege. In our fight we take the given state as our basis; we unite the workers of all nations in the given state; we cannot vouch for any particular path of national development, we are marching to our class goal by *all* possible paths.

But we cannot advance to that goal unless we combat all nationalism, unless we fight for the equality of the workers of all nations. Whether the Ukraine, for example, is destined to form an independent state is a matter that will be determined by a thousand factors, which cannot be foreseen. Without attempting idle *"guesses,"* we firmly uphold what is beyond doubt: the right of the Ukraine to form such a state. We respect this right; we do not uphold the privileges of the Great Russians over the Ukrainians; we *teach* the masses to recognize that right, and to reject the *state* privileges of any nation.

In the leaps which all nations take in the period of bourgeois revolutions, clashes and struggle over the right to a national state are possible and probable. We proletarians declare in advance that we are *opposed* to Great-Russian privileges, and this is what guides our entire propaganda and agitation.

In her quest for "practicalness" Rosa Luxemburg has overlooked the *principal* practical task both of the Great-Russian proletariat and of the proletariat of other nationalities: the task of daily agitation and propaganda against all state and national privileges and for the right, the equal right of all nations to their national state. This task is (at present) our principal task in the national question, for only in this way can we defend the interests of democracy and the alliance of all proletarians of all nations on an equal footing.

This propaganda may be "impractical" from the point of view of the Great-Russian oppressors as well as from the point of view of the bourgeoisie of the oppressed nations (both demand a *definite* "yes" or "no," and accuse the Social-Democrats of being "vague"). In reality it is this propaganda, and only this propaganda, that ensures the really democratic, the really socialist education of the masses. Only such propaganda ensures the greatest chances of national peace in Russia, should she remain a heterogeneous national state, and the most peaceful (and for the proletarian class struggle, harmless) division into separate national states, should the question of such a division arise.

To explain this, the only proletarian policy in the national question, more concretely we shall examine the attitude of Great-Russian

Liberalism towards "self-determination of nations," and the example of the secession of Norway from Sweden.

THE LIBERAL BOURGEOISIE AND THE SOCIALIST OPPORTUNISTS ON THE NATIONAL QUESTION

We have seen that one of Rosa Luxemburg's "trump cards" in her crusade against the program of the Russian Marxists is the following argument: The recognition of the right to self-determination is tantamount to supporting the bourgeois nationalism of the oppressed nations. On the other hand, she says, if by this right we mean nothing more than combating the use of violence against other nations, there is no need to have a special point in the program about it, for Social-Democrats are, in general, opposed to all national oppression and all national inequality.

The first argument, as Kautsky irrefutably proved nearly twenty years ago, is a case of blaming other people for one's own nationalism; for in fearing the nationalism of the bourgeoisie of the oppressed nations, Rosa Luxemburg is *actually* playing into the hands of the Black-Hundred nationalism of the Great Russians! Her second argument is virtually a timid evasion of the question: Does the recognition of national equality include the recognition of the right to secession or not? If it does, then Rosa Luxemburg admits that, in principle, point 9 of our program is correct. If it does not, then she does not believe in national equality. Twists and evasions will not help matters here in the least!

The best way to test the above and all analogous arguments, however, is to study the attitude of the *various classes* of society towards this question. A Marxist must make this test. He must proceed from the objective; he must examine the relations of the classes on this point. Failing to do this, Rosa Luxemburg is guilty of those very sins of metaphysics, abstractions, platitudes, sweeping statements, etc., of which she vainly accuses her opponents.

We are discussing the program of the Marxists in *Russia, i.e.,* of the Marxists of all the nationalities in Russia. Should we not examine the position of the *ruling* classes of Russia?

The position of the "bureaucracy" (we beg to be excused for this inexact term)* and the feudal landlords of the type of our United

* For reasons of the censorship Lenin here uses the term "bureaucracy" instead of "tsarism."—*Ed.*

Nobility is well known. They categorically reject both equality of nationalities and the right to self-determination. They adhere to the old motto of the days of serfdom: autocracy, orthodoxy, nationality —the last term applying only to the Great-Russian nation. Even the Ukrainians have been declared to be "aliens," and even their language is being suppressed.

Let us glance at the Russian bourgeoisie, which was "called" to take part—a very modest part, it is true, but nevertheless some part— in the government, under the "June Third"* legislative and administrative system. There is no need to dilate on the fact that the Octobrists† are really following the Rights in this question. Unfortunately, some Marxists pay much less attention to the position of the Great-Russian liberal bourgeoisie, the Progressives and the Cadets.‡ And yet he who fails to study and ponder over this position will inevitably flounder in abstractions and unsupported statements in discussing the question of the right of nations to self-determination.

Skilled though it is in the art of diplomatically evading direct answers to "unpleasant" questions, *Ryech,* the principal organ of the Constitutional-Democratic Party, was compelled, in its controversy with the *Pravda*§ last year, to make certain valuable admissions.

* "June Third system." On June 3, 1907, the tsarist government dissolved the Second State Duma and published a new election law for a Third Duma which curtailed the already restricted rights of workers and peasants. This day has come to be called the day of the June Third *coup d'état.* The government abrogated the Constitutional rights it had itself proclaimed, prosecuted the Social-Democratic deputies of the Second Duma and sentenced them to hard labor in exile. The June Third *coup d'état* denoted a temporary victory of the counter-revolution and the beginning of the so-called "June Third regime," or the "June Third system" in Russia.—*Ed.*

† Octobrists, Octobrist Party (or the "Alliance of October 17"), represented the interests of big industrial capital and of the big landlords who were managing their estates on a capitalist basis. While ostensibly recognizing the manifesto of October 17 [30], 1905, in which the Tsar, frightened by the Revolution, had promised civil rights to the people, they never had the slightest intention of limiting the powers of tsarism in practice. They gave its foreign and domestic policy their whole-hearted support.—*Ed.*

‡ Cadets, abbreviated name of the Constitutional-Democratic Party.—*Ed.*

§ *Pravda* (*Truth*), legal Bolshevik daily which was first published in St. Petersburg on April 22 (May 5), 1912. Its organizers and leading figures were Lenin and Stalin. The newspaper was constantly harassed by the tsarist government and repeatedly closed down, when it would reappear under a new name such as *Rabochaya Pravda* (*Workers' Truth*), *Proletarskaya Pravda* (*Proletarian Truth*), and the like. After the fall of tsarism, it was published in Petrograd as the organ of the Bolshevik Party; and after the July Days, Stalin succeeded Lenin as the responsible editor.—*Ed.*

The trouble started over the All-Ukraine Students' Congress that was held in Lvov in the summer of 1913. Mr. Mogilyansky, the sworn "Ukrainian expert" or Ukrainian correspondent of *Ryech*, wrote an article in which he heaped the choicest invectives ("delirium," "adventurism," etc.) on the idea that the Ukraine should secede, which Dontsov, a Social-Nationalist, had advocated and the above-mentioned congress had approved.

Rabochaya Pravda, in no way identifying itself with Mr. Dontsov and plainly declaring that he was a Social-Nationalist and that many Ukrainian Marxists did not agree with him, stated that the *tone* of *Ryech*, or, rather, the way *it formulated the question in principle*, was improper and reprehensible for a Great-Russian democrat, or for anyone desiring to pass as a democrat. Let *Ryech* repudiate the Dontsovs if it likes, but from the standpoint of *principle*, a Great-Russian organ of democracy, as it claims to be, cannot be oblivious to *freedom* to secede, the *right* to secede.

A few months later Mr. Mogilyansky, having learned from the Ukrainian newspaper *Shlyakhi*, published in Lvov, of Mr. Dontsov's reply—in the course of which, incidentally, Dontsov had stated that "the chauvinist attacks in *Ryech* have been properly branded [stigmatized?] only in the Russian Social-Democratic press," wrote an "explanation" in *Ryech*, No. 331. This "explanation" consisted of the thrice repeated statement that "criticism of Mr. Dontsov's recipes" "does not mean rejection of the right of nations to self-determination."

"It must be said," wrote Mr. Mogilyansky, "that even 'the right of nations to self-determination' is not a fetish [hear! hear!] that must not be criticized: morbid conditions in the life of nations may give rise to morbid tendencies in national self-determination, and the fact that these are brought to light does not mean that the right of nations to self-determination is rejected."

As you see, this Liberal's talk about a "fetish" is quite in keeping with Rosa Luxemburg's. It was obvious that Mr. Mogilyansky wanted to avoid giving a direct reply to the question: does he recognize the right to political self-determination, *i.e.*, to secession, or not?

Proletarskaya Pravda (No. 4, of December 11, 1913) put this question *point-blank* to Mr. Mogilyansky and to the Constitutional-Democratic *Party*.

Ryech, then (No. 340), published an unsigned, *i.e.*, an official editorial statement replying to this question. This reply can be reduced to the following three points:

1. Point 11 of the program of the Constitutional-Democratic Party

speaks very definitely and clearly of "the right of nations to free *cultural* self-determination."

2. According to *Ryech, Proletarskaya Pravda* "hopelessly confuses" self-determination with separatism, with the secession of particular nations.

3. *"Actually, the Constitutional-Democrats have never pledged themselves to advocate the right of 'nations to secede' from the Russian state."* (See article, "National-Liberalism and the Right of Nations to Self-Determination," in the *Proletarskaya Pravda*, No. 12, December 20, 1913.)

Let us first consider the second point of the statement in *Ryech.* How vividly it shows the Semkovskys, the Liebmans, the Yurkeviches and other opportunists that the hue and cry they have raised about the alleged "vagueness," or "indefiniteness," of the term "self-determination" is *in fact, i.e., from the standpoint of objective class relationships and the class struggle in Russia, a *mere repetition* of the utterances of the Liberal monarchist bourgeoisie!

Proletarskaya Pravda then put the following *three* questions to the enlightened "Constitutional-Democratic" gentlemen on *Ryech:* (1) Do they deny that throughout the history of international democracy, especially since the middle of the nineteenth century, self-determination of nations has been taken to mean precisely political self-determination, the right to form an independent national state? (2) Do they deny that the well-known resolution adopted by the International Socialist Congress in London in 1896 has the same meaning? and (3) Do they deny that Plekhanov, in writing about self-determination as far back as 1902, meant precisely political self-determination? When *Proletarskaya Pravda* put these three questions, *the Cadets shut up!!*

Not a word did they say in reply, for they had nothing to say. They had tacitly to admit that *Proletarskaya Pravda* was absolutely right.

The outcries of the Liberals that the term "self-determination" is vague and that the Social-Democrats "hopelessly confuse" it with secession are nothing more than attempts to *confuse* the issue, to evade admitting a universally established democratic principle. If the Semkovskys, Liebmans, and Yurkeviches were not so ignorant, they would be ashamed to speak to the workers like *Liberals.*

But to proceed. *Proletarskaya Pravda* compelled *Ryech* to admit that in the program of the Constitutional-Democrats the term "cultural" self-determination means in effect the *repudiation* of *political* self-determination.

"Actually, the Constitutional-Democrats have never pledged themselves to advocate the right of 'nations to secede' from the Russian state"—it was not without reason that the *Proletarskaya Pravda* recommended these words from *Ryech* to the *Novoye Vremya** and the *Zemshchina*† as an example of the "loyalty" of our Cadets. Not missing the opportunity of mentioning the "Jews" and of making all kinds of caustic remarks at the expense of the Cadets, the *Novoye Vremya,* in its issue No. 13,563, nevertheless stated:

"What is an axiom of political wisdom among the Social-Democrats" (*i.e.,* the recognition of the right of nations to self-determination, to secession), "is, today, beginning to arouse differences of opinion even in Cadet circles."

By declaring that they "have never pledged themselves to advocate the right of nations to secede from the Russian state," the Cadets, in principle, have taken exactly the same position as the *Novoye Vremya.* This is precisely one of the principles of Cadet *National-Liberalism,* which makes them akin to the Purishkeviches,‡ and is one of the causes of their political dependence, ideological and practical, on the latter. *Proletarskaya Pravda* wrote: "Messrs. the Cadets have studied history and are perfectly well aware of the 'pogrom-like,' to put it mildly, actions to which the exercise of the ancient right of the Purishkeviches to 'arrest and prevent'§ has often led." Although they are perfectly well aware of the feudal source and nature of the omnipotence of the Purishkeviches, the Cadets, nevertheless, are taking their stand *on the basis* of the relations and frontiers created by this very class. Knowing perfectly well how much there is in the relations and frontiers created or fixed by this class that is un-European, anti-European (we would say Asian if this did not sound undeservedly derogatory to the Japanese and Chinese), Messrs. the Cadets, nevertheless, accept them as the limit beyond which they dare not go.

* *Novoye Vremya* (*New Times*), newspaper appearing in St. Petersburg from 1868 to October 1917. In 1876 it became the organ of the reactionary circles of the Court and the bureaucracy. Combatted not only the revolutionary but also the liberal bourgeois movement.—*Ed.*

† *Zemshchina* (*People*), Black-Hundred newspaper appearing in St. Petersburg, 1909-17.—*Ed.*

‡ V. Purishkevich (1870-1920), big landlord, arrant monarchist and reactionary, founder of the Black-Hundred "Alliance of the Russian people."—*Ed.*

§ *"Arrest and prevent"* (literally in Russian "to drag and not to let"); the words are from Gleb Uspensky's story, *The Police Station,* depicting an overzealous provincial policeman, Mymretsov, who, with or without reason, would "drag" people to the police station, or "not let" them go where they wanted to.—*Ed.*

Thus, they are adjusting themselves to the Purishkeviches, cringing to them, fearing to endanger their position, protecting them from the people's movement, from the democracy. As *Proletarskaya Pravda* wrote:

"Actually, this means that they are adjusting themselves to the interests of the feudal lords and to the worst nationalistic prejudices of the dominant nation instead of systematically combating these prejudices."

As men who are familiar with history and claim to be democrats, the Cadets do not even attempt to assert that the democratic movement which today characterizes Eastern Europe and Asia and is striving to change both on the model of the civilized capitalist countries, that this movement must leave intact the boundaries fixed by the feudal epoch, the epoch of the omnipotence of the Purishkeviches and the disfranchisement of wide strata of the bourgeoisie and petty bourgeoisie.

The fact that the question raised in the controversy between the *Proletarskaya Pravda* and *Ryech* was not merely a literary question but one that concerned a real political issue of the day, was proved, among other things, by the last conference of the Constitutional-Democratic Party, held on March 23-25, 1914. In the official report of this conference in *Ryech* (No. 83, of March 26, 1914) we read:

"A particularly lively discussion also took place on national problems. The Kiev deputies, who were supported by N. V. Nekrasov and A. M. Kolyubakin, pointed out that the national question is becoming an important factor that will have to be taken up more resolutely than hitherto. F. F. Kokoshkin pointed out, however" (this "however" is like Shchedrin's "but"—"The ears will never grow higher than the forehead, never!"), "that both the program and past political experience demand that 'elastic formulas' of 'political self-determination of nationalities' should be handled very carefully."

This highly remarkable line of reasoning at the Cadet conference deserves the serious attention of all Marxists and of all democrats. (We will note in parenthesis that the *Kievskaya Mysl*,* which is evidently very well informed and no doubt presents Mr. Kokoshkin's ideas correctly, added that he laid special stress, as a warning to his opponents, of course, on the danger of the "disintegration" of the state.)

The official report in *Ryech* is composed with consummate diplo-

---

* *Kievskaya Mysl* (*Kiev Thought*), liberal bourgeois newspaper appearing in Kiev from 1906 to February 1918.—*Ed.*

matic skill, so as to raise the curtain as little as possible and to conceal as much as possible. Yet, in the main, what happened at the Cadet conference is quite clear. The Liberal bourgeois delegates who were familiar with the state of affairs in the Ukraine, and the "Left" Cadets raised the question of *political* self-determination of nations. Otherwise, there would have been no reason for Mr. Kokoshkin to urge that this "formula" should be "handled carefully."

The Cadet program, with which, naturally, the delegates at the Cadet conference were familiar, speaks *not* of political but of "cultural" self-determination. Hence, Mr. Kokoshkin was *defending* the program *against* the Ukrainian delegates, *against* the Left Cadets; he was defending "cultural" self-determination as *against* "political" self-determination. It is quite obvious that in opposing "political" self-determination, in talking about the danger of the "disintegration of the state," in calling the formula "political self-determination" an *"elastic"* one (just as Rosa Luxemburg does!), Mr. Kokoshkin was defending Great-Russian National-Liberalism against the more "Left" or more democratic elements of the Constitutional-Democratic Party, and against the Ukrainian bourgeoisie.

Mr. Kokoshkin was victorious at the Cadet conference, as is evident from the treacherous little word "however" in the report in *Ryech*. Great-Russian National Liberalism has triumphed among the Cadets. Will not this victory help to clear the minds of those unwise individuals among the Marxists in Russia who, like the Cadets, have also begun to fear the "elastic formulas of political self-determination of nationalities"?

Let us, "however," examine the substance of Mr. Kokoshkin's line of thought. By referring to "past political experience" (*i.e.*, evidently, the experience of 1905, when the Great-Russian bourgeoisie grew alarmed about its national privileges and infected the Cadet Party with its fears), and by talking about the danger of the "disintegration of the state," Mr. Kokoshkin showed that he understood perfectly well that political self-determination can mean nothing else than the right to secede and to form an independent national state. The question is: How should Mr. Kokoshkin's fears be appraised from the democratic standpoint in general, and from/the standpoint of the proletarian class struggle in particular?

Mr. Kokoshkin wants to assure us that recognition of the right to secession would increase the danger of the "disintegration of the state." This is the viewpoint of Constable Mymretsov, whose motto was "arrest and prevent." From the democratic viewpoint, the very opposite is the case: recognition of the right to secession *reduces* the danger of the "disintegration of the state."

Mr. Kokoshkin argues exactly like the nationalists. At their last congress they fiercely attacked the Ukrainian "Mazeppa-ites."* The Ukrainian movement, exclaimed Messrs. Savenko and Co., threatens to weaken the ties between the Ukraine and Russia; for by her Ukrainophilism Austria is strengthening her ties with Ukrainians!! Why Russia cannot try to "strengthen" her ties with the Ukrainians *by the same methods* that Messrs. the Savenkos blame Austria for using, *i.e.,* by granting the Ukrainians freedom to use their own language, self-government, an autonomous Diet, etc., remains unexplained.

The arguments of the Savenkos and Kokoshkins are exactly alike, and they are equally ridiculous and absurd from the purely logical point of view. Is it not clear that the more liberty the Ukrainian nationality enjoys in any particular country, the firmer will its ties with that country be? One would think that this truism cannot be disputed unless one totally abandons all the premises of democracy. And can there be greater freedom of nationality, as such, than freedom to secede, freedom to form an independent national state?

To make this question, which has been so confused by the Liberals (and by those who echo them in their simplicity), a little clearer, we shall cite a very simple example. Let us take the question of divorce. In her article Rosa Luxemburg writes that the centralized democratic state, while conceding autonomy to its constituent parts, should retain the most important branches of legislation, including legislation on divorce, under the jurisdiction of the central parliament. The desire that the central authority of the democratic state should have the power to grant freedom of divorce is quite comprehensible. The reactionaries are opposed to freedom of divorce; they say that this must be "handled carefully," and loudly declare that it means the "disintegration of the family." The democrats, however, believe that the reactionaries are hypocrites, that actually, they are defending the omnipotence of the police and the bureaucracy, the privileges of one sex, and the worst kind of oppression of women. They believe that freedom of divorce will not cause the "disintegration" of family ties but, on the contrary, will strengthen them on a democratic basis, which is the only possible and durable basis in civilized society.

To accuse the supporters of freedom of self-determination, *i.e.,*

* *Ukrainian* Mazeppa-ites, name given to Ukrainian nationalist separatists, after the Ukrainian hetman Mazeppa (1644-1709) who strove to separate the Ukraine from the Moscow state.—*Ed.*

freedom to secede, of encouraging separatism, is as foolish and as hypocritical as accusing the advocates of freedom of divorce of wishing to destroy family ties. Just as in bourgeois society the defenders of privilege and corruption, on which bourgeois marriage rests, oppose freedom of divorce, so, in the capitalist state, repudiation of the right to self-determination, *i.e.*, the right of nations to secede, is tantamount to defending the privileges of the dominating nation and police methods of administration as against democratic methods.

No doubt, the political corruption engendered by the relations prevailing in capitalist society sometimes leads members of parliament and journalists to indulge in frivolous and even in just nonsensical twaddle about a particular nation seceding. But only reactionaries can allow themselves to be frightened (or pretend to be frightened) by such twaddle. Those who stand by democratic principles, *i.e.*, who insist that questions of state must be decided by the people, know very well that there is a very big difference between what the politicians prate about and what the people decide. The people know from daily experience the value of geographical and economic ties and the advantages of a big market and of a big state. They will, therefore, resort to secession only when national oppression and national friction make joint life absolutely intolerable and hinder all economic intercourse. In that case, the interests of capitalist development and of the freedom of the class struggle will be best served by secession.

Thus, from whatever angle we approach Mr. Kokoshkin's arguments they prove to be absolutely absurd and a mockery of the principles of democracy. But there is a modicum of logic in these arguments, the logic of the class interests of the Great-Russian bourgeoisie. Like the majority of the members of the Constitutional-Democratic Party, Mr. Kokoshkin is a guardian of the moneybags of this bourgeoisie. He defends its privileges in general, and its *state* privileges in particular. He defends them hand in hand with Purishkevich, shoulder to shoulder with him, the only difference between them being that Purishkevich puts more faith in the feudal cudgel, while Kokoshkin and Co. realize that this cudgel was badly cracked in 1905, and rely more on bourgeois methods of deceiving the masses, such as frightening the philistines and the peasants with the specter of the "disintegration of the state," deluding them with phrases about combining "national freedom" with the principles established by history, etc.

The Liberals' hostility to the principle of political self-determination of nations can have only one real class meaning, and that is,

35

National-Liberalism, defense of the state privileges of the Great-Russian bourgeoisie. And the opportunists among the Marxists in Russia, who today, under the June Third regime, are strenuously opposing the right of nations to self-determination, the Liquidator Semkovsky, the Bundist Liebman, the Ukrainian petty-bourgeois Yurkevich, are *actually* trailing behind the National-Liberals, corrupting the working class with National-Liberal ideas.

The interests of the working class and of its struggle against capitalism demand complete solidarity and the closest unity of the workers of all nations; they demand strong opposition to the nationalistic policy of the bourgeoisie of every nationality. Hence, Social-Democrats would be equally running counter to proletarian policy and subordinating the workers to the policy of the bourgeoisie if they were to repudiate the right of nations to self-determination, *i.e.,* the right of an oppressed nation to secede, or if they were to support all the national demands of the bourgeoisie of the oppressed nations. It makes no difference to the wage worker whether he is exploited chiefly by the Great-Russian bourgeoisie rather than by the non-Russian bourgeoisie, or by the Polish bourgeoisie rather than the Jewish bourgeoisie, etc. The wage worker who understands his class interests is equally indifferent to the state privileges of the Great-Russian capitalists and to the promises of the Polish or Ukrainian capitalists to set up an earthly paradise when they obtain state privileges. Capitalism is developing and will continue to develop, in one way or another, both in united heterogeneous states and in separate national states.

In any case the wage workers will be exploited. And in order to be able to fight successfully against exploitation, the proletariat must be free of nationalism, must be absolutely neutral, so to speak, in the struggle for supremacy that is going on among the bourgeoisie of the various nations. If the proletariat of any one nation gives the slightest support to the privileges of "its" national bourgeoisie, this will inevitably rouse distrust among the proletariat of the other nation; it will weaken the international class solidarity of the workers and divide them, to the delight of the bourgeoisie. And repudiation of the right to self-determination, or secession, inevitably means, in practice, supporting the privileges of the dominating nation.

We will get even more striking confirmation of this if we take the concrete case of the secession of Norway from Sweden.

THE SECESSION OF NORWAY FROM SWEDEN

Rosa Luxemburg cites this example and discusses it in the following way:

"The latest event in the history of federative relations, the secession of Norway from Sweden—which at the time was hastily caught up by the social-patriotic Polish press (*see* the Cracow *Naprzód**) as a gratifying sign of the strength and progressive nature of the aspirations for state separation—at once provided striking proof that federalism and its concomitant separation are not an expression of progress or democracy. After the so-called Norwegian 'revolution,' which meant that the Swedish king was deposed and compelled to leave Norway, the Norwegians very calmly chose another king, formally rejecting, by a national referendum, the proposal to establish a republic. What the superficial admirers of all national movements and all semblance of independence proclaimed as a 'revolution' was simply a manifestation of peasant and petty-bourgeois particularism, the desire to have their 'own' king for their money instead of one foisted upon them by the Swedish aristocracy, and, consequently, was a movement that had nothing to do with revolution. At the same time, the dissolution of the union between Sweden and Norway showed once again to what extent, in this case too, federation, which had existed until then, was only an expression of purely dynastic interests and, therefore, merely a form of monarchism and reaction. . . ." (*Przeglad.*)

That is literally all that Rosa Luxemburg has to say on this subject!! It must be confessed that it would have been difficult for Rosa Luxemburg to have revealed the hopelessness of her position more vividly than she has done in this case. The question was, and is, whether the Social-Democrats in a mixed national state need a program that recognizes the right to self-determination or to secession. What does the example of Norway, cited by Rosa Luxemburg herself, tell us on this point?

Our author twists and turns, exercises her wit and rails at *Naprzód,* but she does not answer the question!! Rosa Luxemburg speaks about everything under the sun so as *to avoid saying a single word* about the actual point at issue!!

Undoubtedly, in wishing to have their own king for their money, and in rejecting, in a national referendum, the proposal to establish

* *Naprzód* (*Forward*), central organ of the Polish Social-Democratic Party of Galicia and Silesia; first appeared in Cracow in 1892.—*Ed.*

37

a republic, the Norwegian petty-bourgeoisie displayed exceedingly bad philistine qualities. Undoubtedly, *Naprzód* displayed equally bad and equally philistine qualities by failing to notice this. But what has all this to do with the case??

The question under discussion was the right of nations to self-determination and the attitude the Socialist proletariat should adopt towards this right! Why, then, does not Rosa Luxemburg answer this question instead of skirting around it?

It is said that in the eyes of a mouse there is no animal stronger than the cat. In Rosa Luxemburg's eyes there is evidently no animal stronger than the "Fraki." "Fraki" is the popular term for the "Polish Socialist Party," the so-called revolutionary faction, and the Cracow newspaper, the *Naprzód,* shares the views of this "faction." Rosa Luxemburg is so blinded by her fight against the nationalism of this "faction" that everything except the *Naprzód* drops out of sight.

If the *Naprzód* says "yes," Rosa Luxemburg considers it her bounden duty immediately to say "no," without stopping to think that by doing so she does not show that she is independent of the *Naprzód,* but on the contrary, she shows that she is ludicrously dependent on the "Fraki," that she is unable to see things from a somewhat deeper and broader viewpoint than that of the Cracow ant-hill. The *Naprzód,* of course, is a wretched, and by no means a Marxist, organ; but this should not prevent us from properly analyzing the example of Norway, once we have chosen it.

To analyze this example in a Marxist way, we must deal, not with the vices of the awfully terrible "Fraki," but, firstly, with the concrete historical features of the secession of Norway from Sweden, and second, with the tasks the *proletariat* of both countries was confronted with in connection with this secession.

The geographic, economic, and language ties between Norway and Sweden are no less close than those between the Great Russians and many other Slav nations. But the union between Norway and Sweden was not a voluntary one, so that Rosa Luxemburg's reference to "federation" is quite beside the point, and she had recourse to it simply because she did not know what to say. Norway was *ceded* to Sweden by the monarchs during the Napoleonic wars, against the will of the Norwegians; and the Swedes had to send troops into Norway to subjugate her.

Despite the exceptionally extensive autonomy which Norway enjoyed (she had her own parliament, etc.), for many decades after the union there was constant friction between Norway and Sweden, and the Norwegians tried to throw off the yoke of the Swedish aristocracy. At last, in August 1905, they succeeded: the Norwegian parliament resolved that the Swedish king was no longer king of Norway, and in the referendum held later among the Norwegian people, the overwhelming majority (about 200,000 as against a few hundred) voted for complete separation from Sweden. After a short period of indecision, the Swedes resigned themselves to the fact of secession.

This example shows us on what grounds cases of the secession of nations are possible, and actually occur, under the modern economic and political relations, and the *form* secession sometimes assumes under conditions of political freedom and democracy.

Not a single Social-Democrat, unless he wants to profess that political freedom and democracy are matters of indifference to him (and in that case he would naturally cease to be a Social-Democrat), can deny that this example is *practical* proof that it is the *bounden duty* of class-conscious workers to conduct systematic propaganda and prepare the ground for the settlement of conflicts that may arise over the secession of nations not in the "Russian way," but *only in the way* they were settled in 1905 between Norway and Sweden. This is exactly what the demand in the program for the recognition of the right of nations to self-determination means. But Rosa Luxemburg tried to get round a fact that was repugnant to her theory by severely attacking the philistinism of the Norwegian philistines and the Cracow *Naprzód;* for she understood perfectly well that this historical fact *utterly refutes* her contention that the right to self-determination of nations is a "utopia," that it is like the right "to eat from gold plates," etc. Such phrases only express a smug, opportunist faith in the immutability of the present alignment of forces among the nationalities of Eastern Europe.

Let us proceed further. In the question of the self-determination of nations, as in every other question, we are interested, first and foremost, in the self-determination of the proletariat within a given nation. Rosa Luxemburg modestly evaded this question too, for she realized that an analysis of it on the basis of the example of Norway, which she herself chose, would be disastrous for her "theory."

What position did the Norwegian and Swedish proletariat take, and have to take, in the conflict over secession? *After* Norway seceded, the class-conscious workers of Norway would naturally vote

39

for a republic,* and if some Socialists voted otherwise it only goes to show how much stupid, philistine opportunism there sometimes is in the European Socialist movement. There can be no two opinions about that, and we mention this point only because Rosa Luxemburg is trying to obscure the issue by speaking *beside the point.* We do not know whether the Norwegian Socialist program made it obligatory for Norwegian Social-Democrats to hold a particular view on the question of secession. We will assume that it did not, that the Norwegian Socialists left it an open question as to whether the autonomy of Norway gave sufficient scope for freely waging the class struggle, or whether eternal friction and conflicts with the Swedish aristocracy hindered the freedom of economic life. But the fact that it was the duty of the Norwegian proletariat to oppose this aristocracy and to support Norwegian peasant democracy (even with all its philistine limitations) cannot be disputed.

And what about the Swedish proletariat? It is common knowledge that the Swedish landlords, abetted by the Swedish clergy, advocated war against Norway. And since Norway was much weaker than Sweden, since it had already experienced a Swedish invasion and since the Swedish aristocracy carries enormous weight in its own country, this advocacy of war gave rise to a great danger. We may be sure that the Swedish Kokoshkins spent much time and energy in trying to corrupt the minds of the Swedish people by appeals to "handle carefully" the "elastic formulas of political self-determination of nations," by painting horrible pictures of the danger of the "disintegration of the state" and by assuring them that "popular freedom" was compatible with the principles of the Swedish aristocracy. There cannot be the slightest doubt that the Swedish Social-Democrats would have betrayed the cause of socialism and the cause of democracy if they had not fought hard to combat the landlord and "Kokoshkin" ideology and policy, and if they had not demanded *not only* equality of nations in general (to which the Kokoshkins also subscribe) but also the right of nations to self-determination, Norway's freedom to secede.

The fact that the Swedish workers recognized the right of the Norwegians to secede served to *strengthen* the fraternal class solidarity and unity of the Norwegian and Swedish workers. For this

* Since the majority of the Norwegian nation had been in favor of a monarchy while the proletariat had wanted a republic, then, generally speaking, the Norwegian proletariat was confronted with the following alternatives: either revolution, if conditions were ripe for it, or subordination to the will of the majority and prolonged propaganda and agitation work.

convinced the Norwegian workers that the Swedish workers were not infected with Swedish nationalism, that they placed fraternity with the Norwegian proletarians above the privileges of the Swedish bourgeoisie and aristocracy. The dissolution of the ties that had been foisted upon Norway by the monarchs of Europe and the Swedish aristocracy strengthened the ties between the Norwegian and Swedish workers. The Swedish workers proved that in spite of *all* the vicissitudes of bourgeois policy—bourgeois relations may quite possibly cause a repetition of the forcible subjection of the Norwegians to the Swedes!—they will be able to preserve and defend the complete equality and class solidarity of the workers of both nations in the fight against both the Swedish and the Norwegian bourgeoisie.

Incidentally, this reveals how groundless and even frivolous are the attempts the "Fraki" sometimes makes to "use" our disagreements with Rosa Luxemburg against the Polish Social-Democrats. The "Fraki" is not a proletarian, and not a Socialist, but a petty-bourgeois nationalist party, something like Polish Social-Revolutionaries. There never has been, nor could there be any question of unity between the Russian Social-Democrats and this party. On the other hand, not a single Russian Social-Democrat has ever "repented" of the close relations and unity that have been established with the Polish Social-Democrats. The Polish Social-Democrats have rendered great historical service by creating the first really Marxist, really proletarian party in Poland, a country which is thoroughly imbued with nationalistic aspirations and passions. But the service the Polish Social-Democrats have rendered is a great one not because Rosa Luxemburg has talked a lot of nonsense about point 9 of the Russian Marxist program, but despite this sad circumstance.

The question of the "right to self-determination," of course, is not so important for the Polish Social-Democrats as it is for the Russians. It is quite understandable that in their zeal (sometimes a little excessive, perhaps) to combat the nationalistically blinded petty-bourgeoisie of Poland the Polish Social-Democrats should "overdo" it. No Russian Marxist ever thought of blaming the Polish Social-Democrats for being opposed to the secession of Poland. These Social-Democrats err only when, like Rosa Luxemburg, they try to deny the necessity of including the recognition of the right of self-determination in the program of the *Russian* Marxists.

Virtually, this is like attempting to apply what is suitable when measured by Cracow standards to all the peoples and nations inhabiting Russia, including the Great Russians. It means being "Polish

41

nationalists inside out" and not Russian, not international Social-Democrats.

For international Social-Democracy stands for the recognition of the right of nations to self-determination. This is what we shall now proceed to discuss.

THE RESOLUTION OF THE LONDON INTERNATIONAL CONGRESS, 1896

This resolution reads: "The Congress declares that it upholds the full right of self-determination [*Selbstbestimmungsrecht*] of all nations and expresses its sympathy for the workers of every country now suffering under the yoke of military, national, or other despotism; the Congress calls on the workers of all these countries to join the ranks of the class-conscious [*Klassenbewusste*=those who understand their class interests] workers of the whole world and to fight shoulder to shoulder with them for the defeat of international capitalism and for the achievement of the aims of international Social-Democracy."*

As we have already pointed out, our opportunists, Messrs. Semkovsky, Liebman, and Yurkevich, are simply unaware of this resolution. But Rosa Luxemburg is aware of it and quotes the full text, which contains the same expression as that contained in our program, "self-determination."

The question is how does Rosa Luxemburg remove this obstacle which lies in the path of her "original" theory?

Oh, quite simply . . . the whole emphasis lies in the second part of the resolution . . . its declaratory character . . . one would refer to it only under a misapprehension!!

The helplessness and perplexity of our author are simply astounding. Usually, only the opportunists argue that the consistent democratic and Socialist points in the program are merely declarations,

* See the official German report of the London Congress: "*Verhandlungen und Beschlüsse des internationalen sozialistischen Arbeiter und Gewerkschafts-Kongresses zu London, vom. 27. Juli bis 1. August 1896.*" Berlin, 1897, S. 18. [*Proceedings and Decisions of the International Socialist Labour and Trade Union Congress, held in London July 27 to August 1, 1896. Berlin, 1897, p. 18.—Ed.*] A Russian pamphlet has been published containing the decisions of International Congresses, in which the word "self-determination" is wrongly translated as "autonomy."

42

and cravenly avoid an open debate on these points. Not without reason, apparently, has Rosa Luxemburg found herself this time in the deplorable company of Messrs. Semkovsky, Liebman, and Yurkevich. Rosa Luxemburg does not venture to state openly whether she regards the above resolution as correct or erroneous. She wriggles and twists as if counting on the inattentive or ill-informed reader who forgets the first part of the resolution by the time he has started reading the second, or who has never heard of the discussion that took place in the Socialist press *prior to* the London Congress.

However, Rosa Luxemburg is greatly mistaken if she imagines that she can so easily, before the class-conscious workers of Russia, trample upon the resolution of the International on such an important question of principle without even deigning to analyze it critically.

Rosa Luxemburg's point of view was voiced during the discussions which took place prior to the London Congress, mainly in the columns of *Die Neue Zeit,* the organ of the German Marxists, *and this point of view was virtually rejected by the International*! That is the crux of the matter, which the Russian reader particularly must bear in mind.

The debate turned on the question of the independence of Poland. Three points of view were advanced:

1. The point of view of the "Fraki," on whose behalf Hecker spoke. It wanted the International to include in *its* program the demand for the independence of Poland. This proposal was not accepted. This point of view was rejected by the International.

2. Rosa Luxemburg's point of view, *viz.,* that the Polish Socialists must not demand the independence of Poland. This point of view entirely precluded the proclamation of the right of nations to self-determination. This point of view was likewise rejected by the International.

3. The point of view which was then most comprehensively expounded by K. Kautsky in opposing Rosa Luxemburg, when he proved that her materialism was extremely "one-sided." According to this point of view, the International cannot at the present time make the independence of Poland a point in its program; but the Polish Socialists—said Kautsky—are fully entitled to advance such a demand. From the point of view of the Socialists, it is absolutely a mistake to ignore the tasks of national liberation in a situation where national oppression exists.

The resolution of the International reproduces the most essential,

43

the fundamental propositions of this point of view: on the one hand, the absolutely direct, unequivocal recognition of the full right of all nations to self-determination; on the other hand, the equally unambiguous appeal to the workers for *international* unity in their class struggle.

We think that this resolution is absolutely correct, and that for the countries of Eastern Europe and Asia in the beginning of the twentieth century it is precisely this resolution, in both its parts taken as an inseparable whole, that gives the only correct lead to the proletarian class policy in the national question.

We will deal with the three above-mentioned points of view in somewhat greater detail.

It is well known that Karl Marx and Frederick Engels considered that it was the bounden duty of the whole of West European democracy, and still more of Social-Democracy, actively to support the demand for the independence of Poland. For the period of the 1840's, and 1860's, the period of the bourgeois revolutions in Austria and Germany, and the period of the "Peasant Reform" in Russia,* this point of view was quite correct and the only one that was consistently democratic and proletarian. So long as the masses of the people in Russia, and in most of the Slavic countries, were still dormant, so long as *there were no* independent, mass, democratic movements in these countries, the *aristocratic* liberation movement in Poland assumed immense, paramount importance from the point of view, not only of Russian, not only of Slavic, but of European democracy as a whole.†

While this view of Marx was correct for the 40's, 50's and 60's or for the third quarter of the nineteenth century, it has ceased to be correct in the twentieth century. Independent democratic movements, and even an independent proletarian movement, have arisen in most Slavic countries, even in one of the most backward Slavic

---

* Serfdom was abolished in Russia in 1861.—*Ed.*

† It would be a very interesting piece of historical research to compare the position of a Polish aristocrat-rebel in 1863 with that of the Russian democratrevolutionary, Chernyshevsky, who, too (like Marx), knew how to appraise the importance of the Polish movement, and with that of the Ukrainian petty bourgeois Dragomanov, who appeared much later and expressed the point of view of a peasant, so ignorant, so sleepy, and attached so fast to his dungheap, that his legitimate hatred of the Polish aristocracy prevented him from understanding the significance of their struggle for all-Russian democracy. (See Dragomanov, *Historical Poland and Great-Russian Democracy*.) Dragomanov richly deserved the fervent kisses which were subsequently bestowed on him by Mr. P. B. Struve, who by that time had become a National-Liberal.

countries, Russia. Aristocratic Poland has disappeared, yielding place to capitalist Poland. Under such circumstances Poland could not but lose its *exceptional* revolutionary importance. The attempt of the P.P.S. (the Polish Socialist Party, the present-day "Fraki") in 1896 to "fix" for all time the point of view Marx held in a *different epoch* was an attempt to use the *letter* of Marxism against the *spirit* of Marxism. Therefore, the Polish Social-Democrats were quite right when they attacked the extreme nationalism of the Polish petty-bourgeoisie and pointed out that the national question was of secondary importance for Polish workers, when they for the first time created a purely proletarian party in Poland and proclaimed the extremely important principle that the Polish and the Russian workers must maintain the closest alliance in their class struggle.

But did this mean that at the beginning of the twentieth century the International could regard the principle of political self-determination of nations, or the right to secession, as superfluous for Eastern Europe and for Asia? This would have been the height of absurdity, and (theoretically) tantamount to admitting that the bourgeois-democratic reformation of the Turkish, Russian, and Chinese states has been consummated, would have been tantamount (in effect) to opportunism towards despotism.

No. During the period of incipient bourgeois-democratic revolutions in Eastern Europe and Asia, during the period of the awakening and intensification of national movements, during the period of formation of independent proletarian parties, the task of these parties in connection with national policy must be twofold: First, to recognize the right to self-determination for all nations, because the bourgeois-democratic reformation is not yet consummated, because working-class democracy consistently, seriously, and sincerely, and not in a Liberal, Kokoshkin fashion, fights for equal rights for nations, and, second, to maintain the closest, inseparable alliance in the class struggle of the proletarians of all nations in a given state, throughout all the vicissitudes of its history, irrespective of any reshaping of the frontiers of the individual states by the bourgeoisie.

It is precisely this twofold task of the proletariat that the resolution of the International of 1896 formulates. And this is the substance, the underlying principle, of the resolution adopted by the Conference of Russian Marxists held in the summer of 1913. Some people profess to see a "contradiction" in the fact that while point 4 of this resolution, which recognizes the right to self-determination, to secession, seems to "concede" the maximum to nationalism (in reality the recognition of the *right* of *all* nations to self-determination implies the recognition of the maximum of *democracy* and the minimum of nationalism), point 5 warns the workers against the nationalistic slogans of the bourgeoisie of any nation and demands the unity and fusion of the workers of all nations into internationally united proletarian organizations. But this "contradiction" is apparent only to extremely shallow minds which cannot grasp, for instance, why the unity and class solidarity of the Swedish and the Norwegian proletariat were *strengthened* when the Swedish workers upheld Norway's freedom to secede and form an independent state.

UTOPIAN KARL MARX
AND PRACTICAL ROSA LUXEMBURG

While declaring the independence of Poland to be a "utopia" and repeating it *ad nauseam,* Rosa Luxemburg exclaims ironically: Why not raise the demand for the independence of Ireland?

Evidently, "practical" Rosa Luxemburg is unaware of Karl Marx's attitude to the question of the independence of Ireland. It is worth while dwelling upon this, in order to show how a *definite* demand for national independence was analyzed from a really Marxist and not an opportunist standpoint.

It was Marx's custom to "probe the teeth," as he expressed it, of his Socialist acquaintances, testing their intelligence and the strength of their convictions. Having made the acquaintance of Lopatin,* Marx wrote to Engels on July 5, 1870, expressing a highly flattering opinion of the young Russian Socialist but adding at the same time: ". . . *Poland* is his weak point. On this point he speaks quite like an Englishman—say, an English Chartist of the old school—about Ireland."

Marx questions a Socialist belonging to an oppressing nation about his attitude to the oppressed nation and he at once reveals the defect *common* to the Socialists of the dominant nations (the British and the Russian): they fail to understand their Socialist

* G. A. *Lopatin* (1845-1918), a prominent Russian revolutionary; member of the General Council of the First International, Paris; member of the Executive Committee of the Narodnaya Volya Party; was incarcerated in the Schlüsselberg Fortress from which he was released as a result of the 1905 revolution.—*Ed.*

duties towards the downtrodden nations, they echo the prejudices of the "Great Power" bourgeoisie.

Before passing on to Marx's positive declarations on Ireland, we must point out that in general the attitude of Marx and Engels to the national question was strictly critical, and that they recognized its historically relative importance. Thus, Engels wrote to Marx on May 23, 1851, that the study of history was leading him to pessimistic conclusions concerning Poland, that the importance of Poland was temporary, that it would last only until the agrarian revolution in Russia. The role of the Poles in history was one of "brave, quarrelsome stupidity." "And one cannot point to a single instance in which Poland represented progress successfully, even if only in relation to Russia, or did anything at all of historic importance." Russia contains more elements of civilization, education, industry, and of the bourgeoisie than the "Poles, whose whole nature is that of the idle cavalier. . . . What are Warsaw and Cracow compared to St. Petersburg, Moscow, Odessa, etc.!" [2]

Engels had no faith in the success of an insurrection of the Polish aristocracy. But all these thoughts, so full of genius and penetration, by no means prevented Engels and Marx from treating the Polish movement with the most profound and ardent sympathy twelve years later, when Russia was still dormant and Poland was seething.

When drafting the Address of the International in 1864 Marx wrote to Engels (on November 4, 1864) that he had to combat Mazzini's* nationalism, and went on to say: "In so far as international politics come into the address, I speak of countries, not of nationalities, and denounce Russia, not the lesser nations." [3]

Marx had no doubt as to the subordinate position of the national question as compared with the "labor question." But his theory is as far from ignoring the national question as heaven from earth.

The year 1866 arrives. Marx writes to Engels about the "Proudhonist clique"† in Paris which ". . . declares nationalities to be an absurdity and attacks Bismarck and Garibaldi.‡ As polemics against chauvinism their tactics are useful and explicable. But when the believers in Proudhon (my good friends here, Lafargue and Longuet also belong to them) think that all Europe can and should sit quietly

* Giuseppe Mazzini (1805-72), leader of the Italian national revolutionary movement.—*Ed.*

† Pierre Joseph Proudhon (1809-65), ideologist of the petty-bourgeoisie. Marx criticized his theories in *The Poverty of Philosophy,* a polemic against Proudhon's *The Philosophy of Poverty.*—*Ed.*

‡ Giuseppe Garibaldi (1807-1882), revolutionary democratic national liberation leader.—*Ed.*

47

and peacefully on its behind until the gentlemen in France abolish poverty and ignorance . . . they become ridiculous." (Letter of June 7, 1866.)

"Yesterday," Marx writes on June 20, "there was a discussion in the International Council on the present war. . . . The discussion wound up, as was to be expected, with 'the question of nationality' in general and the attitude we should take towards it. . . . The representatives of 'young France' (*non-workers*) came out with the announcement that all nationalities and even nations were 'antiquated prejudices.' Proudhonized Stirnerism. . . . The whole world waits until the French are ripe for a social revolution. . . . The English laughed very much when I began my speech by saying that our friend Lafargue,* etc., who had done away with nationalities, had spoken 'French' to us, *i.e.*, a language which nine-tenths of the audience did not understand. I also suggested that by the negation of nationalities he appeared, quite unconsciously, to understand their absorption into the model French nation."[4]

The conclusion that follows from all these critical remarks of Marx is clear: the working class should be the last to make a fetish of the national question, since the development of capitalism does not necessarily awaken *all* nations to independent life. But to brush aside the mass national movements once they have started and to refuse to support what is progressive in them means, in effect, pandering to *nationalistic* prejudices, *viz.*, recognizing "one's own" as the "model nation" (or, we will add, as the nation possessing the exclusive privilege of forming a state).†

But let us return to the question of Ireland.

Marx's position on this question is most clearly expressed in the following extracts from his letters:

"I have done my best to bring about this demonstration of the British workers in favor of Fenianism. . . .‡ I used to think the separation of Ireland from England impossible. I now think it inevitable, although after the separation there may come *federation*."[5]

* Paul Lafargue (1842-1911), friend and follower of Marx, participant in Paris Commune, and leader of French Socialist movement.—*Ed.*

† See also Marx's letter to Engels of June 3, 1867: ". . . I have learned with real pleasure from the Paris letters to the *Times* about the pro-Polish sentiments of the Parisians as against Russia. . . . M. Proudhon and his little doctrinaire clique are not the French people."

‡ A secret petty-bourgeois revolutionary organization formed in Ireland and America in 1857-58 to struggle for the independence of Ireland.—*Ed.*

This is what Marx wrote to Engels on November 2, 1867. In his letter of November 30 of the same year he added:

". . . what shall we advise the *English* workers? In my opinion they must make the *repeal of the Union"* [*i.e.*, the separation of Ireland from Great Britain] "(in short, the affair of 1783, only democratized and adapted to the conditions of the time) into an article of their *pronunziamento.* This is the only *legal* and therefore only possible form of Irish emancipation which can be admitted in the program of an *English* party. Experience must show later whether a purely personal union can continue to subsist between the two countries. . . .

"What the Irish need is:

"1. Self-government and independence from England;

"2. An agrarian revolution. . . ."[6]

Marx attached great importance to the question of Ireland and he delivered lectures of one-and-a-half-hours' duration at the German Workers' Union on this subject (letter of December 17, 1867).

Engels notes in a letter of November 20, 1868, "the hatred for the Irish among the British workers," and almost a year later (October 24, 1869), returning to this question he writes:

"Il n'y a qu'un pas" (it is only one step) "from Ireland to Russia. . . ." "Irish history shows one how disastrous it is for a nation when it has subjugated another nation. All the abominations of the English have their origin in the Irish Pale. I have still to work through the Cromwellian period, but this much seems certain to me, that things would have taken another turn in England but for the necessity for military rule in Ireland and the creation of a new aristocracy there."[7]

Let us note, by the way, Marx's letter to Engels of August 18, 1869:

"In Posen . . . the Polish workers . . . have brought a strike to a victorious end by the help of their colleagues in Berlin. This struggle against Monsieur le Capital—even in the subordinate form of the strike—is a more serious way of getting rid of national prejudices from that of the bourgeois gentlemen with their peace declamations."[8]

The policy on the Irish question pursued by Marx in the International may be seen from the following:

On November 18, 1869, Marx writes to Engels that he spoke for an hour and a quarter in the Council of the International on the question of the attitude of the British Ministry to the Irish amnesty and proposed the following resolutions:

"Resolved,

"that in his reply to the Irish demands for the release of the imprisoned Irish patriots . . . Mr. Gladstone deliberately insults the Irish nation;

"that he clogs political amnesty with conditions alike degrading to the victims of misgovernment and the people they belong to;

"that having, in the teeth of his responsible position, publicly and enthusiastically cheered on the American slave-holders' rebellion, he now steps in to preach to the Irish people the doctrine of passive obedience;

"that his whole proceedings with reference to the Irish amnesty question are the true and genuine offspring of that *'policy of conquest,'* by the fiery denunciation of which Mr. Gladstone ousted his Tory rivals from office;

"that the *General Council* of the *'International Workingmen's Association'* express their admiration of the spirited, firm and high-souled manner in which the. Irish people carry on their amnesty movement;

"that these resolutions be communicated to all branches of, and workingmen's bodies connected with, the *'International Workingmen's Association'* in Europe and America."[9]

On December 10, 1869, Marx writes that his paper on the Irish question to be read at the Council of the International will be framed on the following lines:

". . . quite apart from all phrases about 'international' and 'humane' *justice for Ireland*—which are to be taken for granted in the *International Council—it is in the direct and absolute interest of the English working class to get rid of their present connection with Ireland*. And this is my most complete conviction, and for reasons which in part I cannot tell the English workers themselves. For a long time I believed that it would be possible to overthrow the Irish regime by English working-class ascendancy. I always expressed this point of view in the *New York Tribune* [an American paper to which Marx contributed for a long time]. Deeper study has now convinced me of the opposite. The English working class will *never accomplish anything* before it has got rid of Ireland. . . . English reaction in England had its roots . . . in the subjugation of Ireland." (Marx's italics.) [10]

Marx's policy on the Irish question should now be quite clear to the readers. Marx, the "utopian," was so "impractical" that he stood for the separation of Ireland, which has not been realized even half a century later. What gave rise to Marx's policy, and was it not a mistake?

At first Marx thought that Ireland would be liberated not by the national movement of the oppressed nation, but by the labor movement of the oppressing nation. Marx did not make an absolute of the national movement, knowing, as he did, that the victory of the working class alone can bring about the complete liberation of all nationalities. It is impossible to estimate beforehand all the possible correlations between the bourgeois liberation movements of the oppressed nations and the proletarian emancipation movement of the oppressing nation (the very problem which today makes the national question in Russia so difficult).

However, matters turned out so that the English working class fell under the influence of the Liberals for a fairly long time, became an appendage of the Liberals and by adopting a Liberal-Labour policy rendered itself effete. The bourgeois liberation movement in Ireland grew stronger and assumed revolutionary forms. Marx reconsidered his view and corrected it. "How disastrous it is for a nation when it has subjugated another nation." The English working class will never be free until Ireland is freed from the English yoke. Reaction in England is strengthened and fostered by the enslavement of Ireland (just as reaction in Russia is fostered by her enslavement of a number of nations!).

And Marx, in proposing in the International a resolution of sympathy with "the Irish nation," "the Irish people" (the clever L.VI. would probably have berated poor Marx for forgetting about the class struggle!), advocates the *separation* of Ireland from England, "although after the separation there may come *federation*."

What were the theoretical grounds for Marx's conclusion? In England the bourgeois revolution had been consummated long ago. But it had not yet been consummated in Ireland; it is being consummated now, after the lapse of half a century, by the reforms of the English Liberals. If capitalism had been overthrown in England as quickly as Marx at first expected, there would have been no room for a bourgeois-democratic and general national movement in Ireland. But since it had arisen, Marx advised the English workers to support it, to give it a revolutionary impetus and lead it to a final issue in the interests of *their own* liberty.

The economic ties between Ireland and England in the 1860's were, of course, even closer than Russia's present ties with Poland, the Ukraine, etc. The "impracticability" and "impossibility" of the separation of Ireland (if only owing to geographical conditions and England's immense colonial power) were quite obvious. While, in principle, an enemy of federalism, Marx in this instance agrees also

51

to federation,* *so long as* the emancipation of Ireland is achieved in a revolutionary and not in a reformist way, through the movement of the mass of the people of Ireland supported by the working class of England. There can be no doubt that only such a solution of the historical problem would be in the best interests of the proletariat and most favorable for rapid social development.

Things turned out differently. Both the Irish people and the English proletariat proved to be weak. Only now, through the miserable deals between the English Liberals and the Irish bourgeoisie, is the Irish problem *being solved* (the example of Ulster shows with what difficulty) through the land reform (with compensation) and autonomy (not introduced so far). Well then? Does it follow that Marx and Engels were "utopians," that they advanced "impossible" national demands, that they allowed themselves to be influenced by the Irish petty-bourgeois nationalists (there is no doubt about the petty-bourgeois nature of the Fenian movement), etc.?

No. In the Irish question too Marx and Engels pursued a consistently proletarian policy, which really educated the masses in the spirit of democracy and socialism. Only such a policy could have saved both Ireland and England from a half a century of delay in the introduction of the necessary reforms, and could have prevented these reforms from being mutilated by the Liberals to please the reactionaries.

The policy of Marx and Engels in the Irish question serves as a splendid example (which retains immense *practical* importance to the present time) of the attitude the proletariat of the oppressing nations should adopt towards national movements. It serves as a warning against that "servile haste" with which the philistines of all countries, colors, and languages hurry to declare "utopian" the idea of changing the frontiers of states that have been established by the violence and privileges of the landlords and bourgeoisie of one nation.

---

* By the way, it is not difficult to see why, from a Social-Democratic point of view, the right of "self-determination" means *neither* federation *nor* autonomy. (Although, speaking in the abstract, both come under the category of "self-determination.") The right to federation is, in general, an absurdity, since federation is a two-sided contract. It goes without saying that Marxists cannot place the defense of federalism in general in their program. As far as autonomy is concerned, Marxists defend not "the right to" autonomy but autonomy *itself,* as a general, universal principle of a democratic state with a mixed national composition, with sharp differences in geographical and other conditions. Consequently, the recognition of the "right of nations to autonomy" is as absurd as the "right of nations to federation."

If the Irish and English proletariat had not accepted Marx's policy, and had not taken the separation of Ireland as their slogan, they would have displayed the worst sort of opportunism; they would have shown that they were oblivious to their duties as democrats and socialists, and would have yielded to *English* reaction and to the *English* bourgeoisie.

THE 1903 PROGRAM AND ITS LIQUIDATORS

Copies of the minutes of the 1903 congress, at which the program of the Russian Marxists was adopted, have become a rarity, so that the overwhelming majority of the active workers in the labor movement today are unacquainted with the motives that underlie the various points of the program (the more so since not all the literature relevant thereto enjoys the blessings of legality. . .). It is therefore necessary to analyze the debate that took place at the 1903 congress on the question that interests us.

Let us state first of all that however meager the Russian Social-Democratic literature on the "right of nations to self determination" may be, it, nevertheless, clearly shows that this right was always understood to mean the right to secession. The Semkovskys, Liebmans and Yurkeviches who doubt this and declare that point 9 is "vague," etc., do so only because of their extreme ignorance or carelessness. As far back as 1902, Plekhanov, in *Zarya,** defending "the right to self-determination" in the draft program, wrote that this demand, while not obligatory for the bourgeois democrats, is *"obligatory* for the Social-Democrats."

"If we were to forget or hesitate to advance it," wrote Plekhanov, "for fear of offending the national prejudices of the present generation of the Great Russians, the call . . . 'workers of all countries, unite!' on our lips would become a brazen lie. . . ."

This is a very apt characterization of the fundamental argument in favor of the point under consideration; so apt that it is not surprising that the critics of our program who have "forgotten their kin" have been timidly avoiding it. The renunciation of this point, no matter for what motives, is *really* a "shameful" concession to *Great-Russian* nationalism. But why Great-Russian, when it is a question of the right of *all* nations to self-determination? Because

* *Zarya* (*Dawn*), theoretical journal of the Russian Social-Democrats, published in 1901-02 in Stuttgart.—*Ed.*

53

it refers to secession *from* the Great Russians. In the interests of the *unity of the proletarians,* in the interests of their class solidarity, we must recognize the right of *nations* to *secession*—that is what Plekhanov admitted in the words quoted above fourteen years ago. Had our opportunists pondered over this they would probably not have talked so much nonsense about self-determination.

At the 1903 congress, which adopted the draft program that Plekhanov advocated, the main work was done in the *program commission.* Unfortunately, no minutes were taken; they would have been particularly interesting on this point for it was *only* in the commission that the representatives of the Polish Social-Democrats, Warszawski and Hanecki, tried to defend their view and to dispute the "recognition of the right to self-determination." The reader who took the trouble to compare their arguments (expounded in the speech by Warszawski and in his and Hanecki's declaration, pp. 134-36 and 388-90 of the congress minutes) with those Rosa Luxemburg advanced in her Polish article, which we have analyzed, would find that they are quite identical.

How were these arguments treated by the program commission of the Second Congress, where Plekhanov, more than anyone else, attacked the Polish Marxists? These arguments were mercilessly ridiculed! The absurdity of proposing to the Marxists *of Russia* that they delete the recognition of the right of nations to self-determination was demonstrated so clearly and vividly that the Polish Marxists *did not even venture to repeat their arguments at the full meeting of the Congress!!* Convinced of the hopelessness of their case at the supreme assembly of Great-Russian, Jewish, Georgian, and Armenian Marxists, they left the Congress.

This historic episode is naturally of very great importance for everyone who is seriously interested in *his* program. The fact that the arguments of the Polish Marxists suffered utter defeat in the program commission of the congress, and that the Polish Marxists gave up the attempt to defend their views at the full meeting of the congress is very significant. It is not without reason that Rosa Luxemburg "modestly" kept silent about it in her article in 1908; apparently the recollection of the congress was too unpleasant! She also kept quiet about the ridiculously inept proposal made by Warszawski and Hanecki in 1903, on behalf of all the Polish Marxists, to "amend" point 9 of the program, a proposal which neither Rosa Luxemburg nor the other Polish Social-Democrats have ventured (or will venture) to repeat.

54

But although Rosa Luxemburg, concealing her defeat in 1903, kept quiet about these facts, those who take an interest in the history of their party will take pains to ascertain the facts and ponder over their significance.

On leaving the 1903 congress Rosa Luxemburg's friends submitted the following statement: ". . . We propose that point 7" (now point 9) "of the draft program read as follows: Point 7. *Institutions guaranteeing full freedom of cultural development to all nations incorporated in the state*" (p. 390 of the minutes).

Thus, the Polish Marxists then propounded views on the national question that were so vague that *instead of* self-determination they actually proposed the notorious "cultural-national autonomy," under another name.

This sounds almost incredible, but unfortunately it is a fact. At the congress itself, although it was attended by five Bundists with five votes, and three Caucasians* with six votes, not counting Kostrov's consulting voice, not a *single* vote was cast for the *deletion* of the point about self-determination. Three votes were cast for the proposal to add to this point "cultural-national autonomy" (in favor of Goldblatt's formula: "the establishment of institutions guaranteeing to the nations complete freedom of cultural development") and four votes for Lieber's formula ("the right of nations to freedom in their cultural development").

Now that a Russian Liberal party, the Constitutional-Democratic Party, has appeared on the scene, we know that in *its* program the political self-determination of nations has been replaced by "cultural self-determination." Thus, Rosa Luxemburg's Polish friends were so successful in *"combating"* the nationalism of the P.P.S. that they proposed to substitute a *Liberal* program for the Marxist program! And in the same breath they accused our program of being opportunist; no wonder this accusation was received with laughter in the Program Commission of the Second Congress!

How was "self-determination" understood by the delegates at the Second Congress, of whom, as we have seen, *not a single one* was opposed to "self-determination of nations"?

The following three extracts from the minutes provide the answer:

---

* *Caucasians,* delegates representing the Social-Democratic organizations of the Caucasus, headed by N. Jordania (Kostrov). On the national question they associated themselves with the Bundists and Russian Mensheviks.—*Ed.*

"Martynov* is of the opinion that the term 'self-determination' should not be given a broad interpretation; it merely means the right of a nation to set itself up as a separate political entity and not regional self-government" (p. 171).

Martynov was a member of the program commission in which the arguments of Rosa Luxemburg's friends were repudiated and ridiculed. Martynov was then "an Economist," a rabid opponent of *Iskra,†* and had he expressed an opinion which was not shared by the majority of the program commission he would certainly have been repudiated.

Goldblatt, a Bundist, was the first to speak when the congress, after the commission had finished its work, discussed point 8 (present point 9) of the program.

Goldblatt said: "Nothing can be said against the 'right to self-determination.' When a nation is fighting for independence, it should not be opposed. If Poland refuses to enter legal marriage with Russia, she should not be compelled to, as Plekhanov put it. I agree with this opinion within these limits" (pp. 175-76).

Plekhanov did not speak at all on this subject at the full meeting of the congress. Goldblatt repeated what Plekhanov had said in the program commission, where the "right to self-determination" had been explained in a simple and detailed manner to mean the right to secession. Lieber, who spoke after Goldblatt, remarked: "Of course, if any nationality finds that it cannot live within the frontiers of Russia, the party will not place any obstacles in its way" (p. 176).

The reader will see that at the Second Congress of the party, which adopted the program, there were no two opinions about self-determination meaning "only" the right to secession. Even the Bundists assimilated this truth at that time, and only in our deplorable times of continued counter-revolution and all sorts of "apostasy" can we find people who, bold in their ignorance, declare that the program is "vague." But before devoting time to these sorry "quasi-Social-

---

* A. C. Martynov (1865-1935), one of the leaders of the Economists and Mensheviks. Joined the Communist Party of the Soviet Union in 1923.—*Ed.*

†*Iskra (Spark)*, first all-Russian newspaper of the revolutionary Marxists, founded by Lenin. Published abroad, it came out December, 1900, and was distributed illegally in Russia. The Leninist, Bolshevik *Iskra* played an immense historical role in preparing the foundation of an independent political party of the Russian proletariat. In November, 1903, soon after the Second Congress of the Russian Social-Democratic Labor Party, the newspaper came under the control of the Mensheviks.—*Ed.*

Democrats," let us first finish with the attitude of the Poles to the program.

They came to the Second Congress (1903) declaring that unity was necessary and urgent. But they left the congress after their "reverse" in the program commission, and their *last word* was their written statement, printed in the minutes of the congress, containing the above-mentioned proposals to *substitute* cultural-national autonomy for self-determination.

In 1906 the Polish Marxists joined the party, and neither upon joining nor afterwards (neither at the congress of 1907, nor at the conferences of 1907 and 1908, nor at the plenum of 1910) *did they once introduce* a single proposal to amend point 9 of the Russian program!

This is a fact.

And despite all phrases and assurances, this fact definitely proves that Rosa Luxemburg's friends regarded this question as having been settled by the debate in the program commission of the Second Congress as well as by the decision of that congress; that they tacitly acknowledged their mistake and corrected it by joining the party in 1906, after they had left the congress in 1903, without having once tried through *party* channels, to raise the question of amending point 9 of the program.

Rosa Luxemburg's article appeared over her signature in 1908—of course, no one ever took it into his head to deny the right of party writers to criticize the program—and *since* this article was written not a *single* official body of the Polish Marxists has raised the question of revising point 9.

Hence, Trotsky is rendering certain admirers of Rosa Luxemburg a very clumsy service when he writes, in the name of the editors of *Borba,* in No. 2 of that publication (March, 1914): ". . . The Polish Marxists consider that 'the right to national self-determination' is entirely devoid of political content and should be deleted from the program" (p. 25).

The obliging Trotsky is more dangerous than an enemy! Trotsky could produce *no* proof except "private conversations" (*i.e.,* simply gossip, on which Trotsky always subsists) for classifying "Polish Marxists" in general as supporters of every article that Rosa Luxemburg writes. Trotsky represented the "Polish Marxists" as people without honor and conscience, incapable of respecting even their own convictions and the program of their party. Obliging Trotsky.

In 1903, when the representatives of the Polish Marxists left the Second Congress *because* of the right to self-determination, Trotsky was entitled to say that they considered that this right was devoid of content and should be deleted from the program.

But after this the Polish Marxists *joined* the party which possessed such a program, and not once have they brought in a motion to amend it.*

Why did Trotsky withhold these facts from the readers of his journal? Only because he finds it advantageous to speculate on provoking disagreements between the Polish and the Russian opponents of Liquidationism and on deceiving the Russian workers on the question of the program.

Trotsky has never yet held a firm opinion on any important question relating to Marxism. He always manages to "creep into the chinks" of this or that difference of opinion, and desert one side for the other. At this moment he is in the company of the Bundists and the Liquidators. And these gentlemen do not stand on ceremony as far as the party is concerned.

Listen to the Bundist Liebman.

"When, fifteen years ago," writes this gentleman, "the Russian Social-Democrats included the point about the right of every nationality to 'self-determination' in their program, everyone [!!] asked himself: what does this fashionable—[!!] term really mean? No answer was forthcoming [!!]. This word was left [!!] enveloped in fog. Indeed, it was difficult at the time to dissipate that fog. The time had not yet come when this point could be made concrete— they used to say at the time—let it remain enveloped in fog—[!!] for the time being and life itself will indicate what content is to be put into this point."

Isn't this "ragamuffin"† mocking at the party program magnificent? And why is he mocking? Only because he is a complete ignoramus who has never learned anything, who has not even read anything on party history, but who simply happened to drop into a Liquidationist environment, where it is "the thing" to be blasé on the question of the party and everything it stands for.

In Pomyalovsky's novel, a student brags of having "spat into the

* We are informed that at the summer conference of the Russian Marxists in 1913, the Polish Marxists attended with *only* a voice but no vote and did not vote at all on the right to self-determination (to secession); they declared that they were opposed to this right in general. Of course, they had a perfect right to act in this way, and, as hitherto, to agitate in Poland against her secession. But this is not quite what Trotsky is saying; for the Polish Marxists did not demand the "deletion" of point 9 "from the program."

† A character in Saltykov-Shchedrin's sketch "In Foreign Lands."—*Ed.*

barrel of sauerkraut."* Messrs. the Bundists go even further. They put up the Liebmans so that these gentlemen may publicly spit into their own barrel. What do the Liebmans care about the fact that an International Congress has passed a decision, that at the congress of their own party two representatives of their own Bund proved that they were quite able (and what "severe" critics and determined enemies of *Iskra* they were!) to understand the meaning of "self-determination" and even agreed to it? And would it not be easier to dissolve the party if the "party writers" (don't laugh) treated the history and the program of the party in seminary student fashion?

Here is a second "ragamuffin," Mr. Yurkevich of *Dzvin*.† Mr. Yurkevich has evidently seen the minutes of the Second Congress, for he cites Plekhanov's words, as repeated by Goldblatt, and shows that he is aware of the fact that self-determination can only mean the right to secession. This, however, does not prevent him from spreading slander among the Ukrainian petty bourgeoisie about the Russian Marxists, alleging that they are in favor of the "state integrity" of Russia. (No. 7-8, 1913, p. 83, etc.) Of course, the Yurkeviches could not have invented a better method than this for alienating the Ukrainian democrats from the Great-Russian democrats. And such alienation is in line with the whole policy of the group of writers on *Dzvin*, who advocate the *segregation* of the Ukrainian workers in a *separate* national organization!‡

It is quite appropriate, of course, for a group of nationalist philistines who are splitting the ranks of the proletariat—and such precisely is the objective role of *Dzvin*—to disseminate such hopeless confusion on the national question. It goes without saying that the Yurkeviches and Liebmans, who are "terribly" offended when they are called "near-party men," do not say a word, not a single word, as to how *they* would like the problem of the right of secession to be solved in the program.

Here is the third and principal "ragamuffin" Mr. Semkovsky, who in the columns of a Liquidationist newspaper, with a Great-Russian

* The reference is to a well-known novel by N. Pomyalovsky entitled *Sketches of a Seminary*, exposing the stupid system of training and the atrocious customs prevailing in Russian religious schools during the fifties and sixties of the last century.—*Ed.*

† *Dzvin* (*The Peal*), Menshevik journal published in Ukrainian; appeared in 1913-14.—*Ed.*

‡ See particularly Mr. Yurkevich's preface to Mr. Levinsky's book *Outline of the Development of the Ukrainian Working-Class Movement in Galicia*, Kiev, 1914.

audience before him, rails at point 9 of the program and at the same time declares that: he "for certain reasons does not approve of the proposal" to delete this point!! This is incredible, but it is a fact.

In August, 1912, the conference of the Liquidators officially raised the national question. For a year and a half not a single article has appeared on the question of point 9 except for the one written by Mr. Semkovsky. And in this article the author *repudiates* the program, because "for *certain* reasons" (is it a secret disease?) he "does not approve" of the proposal to amend it!! We would lay a wager that it would be difficult to find anywhere in the world similar examples of opportunism, and worse than opportunism, of the renunciation of the party, of its liquidation.

One instance will suffice to show what Semkovsky's arguments are like:

"What are we to do," he writes, "if the Polish proletariat desires to fight side by side with the entire Russian proletariat, within the limits of a single state, while the reactionary classes of Polish society, on the contrary, desire to separate Poland from Russia and in a referendum obtain a majority of votes in favor of secession? Should we Russian Social-Democrats in the central parliament vote together with our Polish comrades *against* secession, or—in order not to violate the 'right to self-determination'—vote *for* secession?" (*Novaya Rabochaya Gazeta** [New Workers' Gazette], No. 71).

From this it is evident that Mr. Semkovsky does not even understand *what the discussion is about!* It did not occur to him that the right to secession presupposes the settlement of the question not by the central parliament, but by the parliament (diet, referendum, etc.) of the *seceding* region.

The childish perplexity over the question—"What are we to do" if under democracy the majority is for reaction?—serves to screen the question of real, actual, live politics, when *both* the Purishkeviches *and* the Kokoshkins consider the very idea of secession as criminal! Probably, the proletarians of *all* Russia ought not to fight the Purishkeviches and the Kokoshkins today, but leave them alone and fight the reactionary classes of Poland!

Such is the incredible nonsense that is written in the organ of the Liquidators, of which Mr. L. Martov is one of the ideological leaders, the same L. Martov who drafted the program and got it carried in 1903, and even subsequently wrote in favor of the right

* Newspaper of the Menshevik Liquidators; appeared in St. Petersburg, 1913-14.—*Ed.*

60

of secession. Apparently L. Martov is now arguing according to the rule:

> *No clever man required there;*
> *Better send Read,*
> *And I shall wait and see.**

He sends Read-Semkovsky, and allows our program to be distorted and endlessly confused in a daily paper before new readers, who are unacquainted with our program.

Yes, Liquidationism has gone a long way—even very many prominent ex-Social-Democrats have not a trace of party spirit left in them. Rosa Luxemburg cannot, of course, be put on a par with the Liebmans, Yurkeviches and Semkovskys, but the fact that it is precisely people of this kind who seize upon her mistake shows with particular clarity the opportunism she has lapsed into.

CONCLUSION

To sum up:

From the point of view of the theory of Marxism in general the question of the right of self-determination presents no difficulties. No one can seriously dispute the London resolution of 1896, or the fact that self-determination implies only the right to secession, or the fact that the formation of independent national states is the tendency of all bourgeois-democratic revolutions.

The difficulty is created to a certain extent by the fact that in Russia the proletariat of both oppressed and oppressing nations are fighting and must fight side by side. The task is to preserve the unity of the class struggle of the proletariat for socialism, to resist all the bourgeois and Black-Hundred nationalist influences. Among the oppressed nations the separate organization of the proletariat as an independent party sometimes leads to such a bitter struggle against the nationalism of the respective nation that the perspective becomes distorted and the nationalism of the oppressing nation is forgotten.

But this distortion of the perspective cannot last long. The experience of the joint struggle of the proletarians of various nations has demonstrated only too plainly that we must formulate political questions not from the "Cracow," but from the all-Russian point of view. And in all-Russian politics it is the Purishkeviches and the Kokoshkins who rule. Their ideas are predominant, their perse-

* Quoted from a soldiers' song of the period of the Crimean War, written by Leo Tolstoy. An allusion to the battle of the Chornaya River on August 4, 1855.—*Ed.*

cution of alien races for "separatism," for their *thinking* about secession, is being preached and practised in the Duma, in the schools,
in the churches, in the barracks, and in hundreds and thousands of
newspapers. It is this Great-Russian poison of nationalism that is
contaminating the entire all-Russian political atmosphere. It is the
misfortune of a nation, which, in subjugating other nations, is
strengthening reaction throughout Russia. The memories of 1849
and 1863* form a living political tradition, which, unless great storms
sweep the country, threatens to hamper every democratic and
especially every Social-Democratic movement for many decades.

There can be no doubt that, however natural the point of view of
certain Marxists of the oppressed nations (whose "misfortune" is
sometimes that the masses of the population are blinded by the idea
of "their" national liberation) may appear sometimes, *in reality* the
objective alignment of class forces in Russia makes refusal to advocate the right of self-determination tantamount to the worst opportunism, to the contamination of the proletariat with the ideas of the
Kokoshkins. And in substance, these ideas are the ideas and the
policy of the Purishkeviches.

Therefore, while Rosa Luxemburg's point of view could at first
be excused as being superficially Polish, "Cracow" narrow-mindedness,† at the present time, when nationalism and, above all
governmental Great-Russian nationalism, has grown stronger everywhere, when policy is being shaped by this *Great-Russian* nationalism, such narrow-mindedness becomes inexcusable. In fact, it is
seized upon by the opportunists of *all* nations who fight shy of the
idea of "storms" and "leaps," believe that the bourgeois-democratic
revolution is over, and yearn for the Liberalism of the Kokoshkins.

Great-Russian nationalism, like any other nationalism, passes
through various phases, according to the classes that are supreme in
the bourgeois country at the time. Before 1905 we knew almost
exclusively national reactionaries. After the revolution *National
Liberals* arose in our country.

* The reference is to the suppression in 1849 of the Hungarian Revolution
with the aid of the troops sent by Tsar Nicholas I, and the suppression of the
Polish uprising in 1863 by the tsarist government.—*Ed*.

† It is easy to understand that the recognition by the Marxists of the *whole
of Russia,* and first and foremost by the Great Russians, of the *right* of
nations to secede in no way precludes *agitation* against secession by Marxists
of a particular *oppressed* nation, just as the recognition of the right to
divorce does not preclude agitation against divorce in a particular case. We
think, therefore, that an ever-increasing number of Polish Marxists will laugh
at the non-existent "contradiction" which is now being "hashed up" by
Semkovsky and Trotsky.

In our country this is virtually the position adopted both by the Octobrists and by the Cadets (Kokoshkin), *i.e.,* by the whole of the present-day bourgeoisie. And later on, Great-Russian National Democrats will *inevitably* appear. Mr. Peshekhonov, one of the founders of the "Popular Socialist" Party, expressed this point of view when (in the issue of *Russkoye Bogatstvo** for August 1906) he appealed for caution in regard to the nationalist prejudices of the peasants. However much others may slander us Bolsheviks and declare that we "idealize" the peasant, we always have made and always will make a clear distinction between peasant intelligence and peasant prejudice, between peasant strivings for democracy and opposition to Purishkevich, and peasant strivings to make peace with the priest and the landlord.

Even now, and probably for a fairly long time to come, proletarian democracy must reckon with the nationalism of the Great-Russian peasants (not in the sense of making concessions to it, but in the sense of combating it).† The awakening of nationalism among the oppressed nations, which became so pronounced after 1905 (let us recall, say, the group of "Autonomists-Federalists" in the First Duma, the growth of the Ukrainian movement, of the Moslem movement, etc.), will inevitably cause the intensification of nationalism among the Great-Russian petty bourgeoisie in town and country. The slower the democratization of Russia, the more persistent, brutal, and bitter will be national persecution and quarreling among the bourgeoisie of the various nations. The particularly reactionary spirit of the Russian Purishkeviches will at the same time engender (and strengthen) "separatist" tendencies among the various oppressed nationalities which sometimes enjoy far greater freedom in the neighbouring states.

* *Russkoye Bogatstvo (Russian Wealth)*, monthly Populist journal.—*Ed.*

† It would be interesting to trace the changes that take place in Polish nationalism, for example, in its process of transformation from aristocratic nationalism into bourgeois nationalism and then into peasant nationalism. Ludwig Bernhard, in his book *Das polnische Gemeinwesen im preussischen Staat [The Polish Community in the Prussian State]* (there is a Russian translation), sharing the view of a German Kokoshkin, describes a very characteristic phenomenon: the formation of a sort of "peasant republic" by the Poles in Germany in the form of a close alliance of the various cooperatives and other associations of the *Polish* peasants in their struggle for nationality, for religion, for "Polish" land. German oppression has welded the Poles together, segregated them, first awakening the nationalism of the aristocracy, then of the bourgeois, and finally of the peasant masses (especially after the campaign the Germans inaugurated in 1873 against the Polish language in schools). Things are moving in the same direction in Russia, and not only in regard to Poland.

Such a state of affairs sets the proletariat of Russia a twofold, or, rather, a two-sided task: first, to fight against all nationalism and, above all, against Great Russian nationalism; to recognize not only complete equality of rights for all nations in general, but also equality of rights as regards forming an independent state, *i.e.*, the right of nations to self-determination, to secession. And second, precisely in the interests of the successful struggle against the nationalism of all nations in *any* form, it sets the task of preserving the unity of the proletarian struggle and of the proletarian organizations, of amalgamating these organizations into an international association, in spite of the bourgeois strivings for national segregation.

Complete equality of rights for all nations; the right of nations to self-determination; the amalgamation of the workers of all nations —this is the national program that Marxism, the experience of the whole world, and the experience of Russia, teaches the workers.

This article was already set up when I received No. 3 of *Nasha Rabochaya Gazeta (Our Workers' Gazette)*, where Mr. Vl. Kossovsky writes as follows about the recognition of the right of self-determination for all nations:

"Taken over mechanically from the resolution of the First Congress of the [Social-Democratic] Party (1898), which in turn had borrowed it from the decisions of International Socialist Congresses. it, as is evident from the debate, was given the same meaning at the 1903 congress as was put into it by the Socialist International, *viz.*, political self-determination, *i.e.*, the self-determination of nations in the direction of political independence. Thus, the formula: national self-determination, which implies the right to territorial separation, does not affect the question of how national relations *within* a given state organism should be regulated for nationalities that cannot or have no desire to leave the present state."

It is evident from this that Mr. Vl. Kossovsky has had in his possession the minutes of the Second Congress of 1903 and perfectly well understands the real (and only) meaning of the term self-determination. Compare this with the fact that the editors of the Bund newspaper *Zeit (The Times)* put up Mr. Liebman to jeer at the program and to declare that it is vague!! Queer "party" ethics among these Bundists. . . . Why Kossovsky declares that the Congress took over the principle of self-determination *mechanically,* "Allah alone knows." Some people "want to object," but how, why and wherefore, they do not know.

Prosveshcheniye (Enlightenment) Nos. 4, 5, and 6, 1914.
Collected Works, Vol. XX, Fourth Russian Edition.

Self-Determination of Nations

The most widespread deception of the people by the bourgeoisie in the present war consists in hiding its predatory aims under an ideology of "national liberation." The English promise freedom to Belgium, the Germans to Poland, etc. As we have seen, this is in reality a war of the oppressors of the majority of the nations of the world for deepening and widening such oppression.

The Socialists cannot reach their great aim without fighting against every form of national oppression. They must therefore unequivocally demand that the Social-Democrats of the *oppressing* countries (of the so-called "great" nations in particular) should recognize and defend the right of the *oppressed* nations to self-determination in the political sense of the word, *i.e.,* the right to political separation. A Socialist of a great nation or a nation possessing colonies who does not defend this right is a chauvinist.

To defend this right does in no way mean to encourage the formation of small states, but on the contrary it leads to a freer, more fearless and therefore wider and more universal formation of larger governments and unions of governments—a phenomenon more advantageous for the masses and more in accord with economic development.

On the other hand, the Socialists of the *oppressed* nations must unequivocally fight for complete unity of the *workers* of both the oppressed and the oppressor nationalities (which also means organizational unity). The idea of a lawful separation between one nationality and the other (the so-called "national cultural autonomy" of Bauer and Renner*) is a reactionary idea.

Imperialism is the period of an increasing oppression of the nations of the whole world by a handful of "great" nations; the struggle for a Socialist international revolution against imperialism is therefore impossible without the recognition of the right of nations to self-determination. "No people oppressing other peoples can be free" (Marx and Engels).† No proletariat reconciling itself to the least violation by "its" nation of the rights of other nations can be Socialist.

Written August, 1915.
Collected Works, Vol. XVIII, pp. 235-36.

* Austrian Social-Democratic leaders.—*Ed.*
† Engels in *Volksstaat,* 1874, No. 69—*Ed.*

The Revolutionary Proletariat and the Right

of Nations to Self-Determination

The Zimmerwald Manifesto,* like the majority of the programs of the Social-Democratic parties or their resolutions on tactics, proclaims the right of nations to self-determination. Comrade Parabellum, in Nos. 252 and 523 of the *Berner Tagwacht*,† declares the "struggle for the non-existent right to self-determination" to be illusory; this struggle he contrasts with a "revolutionary mass struggle of the proletariat against capitalism," at the same time asserting that "we are against annexations" (this assertion is repeated five times in Comrade Parabellum's article), and against all "national acts of violence."

The arguments in favor of Comrade Parabellum's position reduce themselves to the assertion that all national problems of the present, like those of Alsace-Lorraine, Armenia, etc., are problems of imperialism; that capital has outgrown the framework of national states; that it is impossible to turn the wheel of history backward to the antiquated ideal of national states, etc.

Let us see whether Comrade Parabellum's arguments are correct.

First of all, it is Comrade Parabellum who looks backward and not forward when, at the beginning of his campaign against the acceptance by the working class "of the ideal of a national state," he directs his glance towards England, France, Italy, Germany, *i.e.,* countries where the national movement for liberation is a thing of the past, and not towards the Orient, Asia, Africa, the colonies,

---

* The Manifesto adopted at the first international conference of representatives of Socialist parties and groups opposed to the imperialist war of 1914-18 held at Zimmerwald, Switzerland, in 1915. A Left grouping led by Lenin was formed at this conference.—*Ed.*

† Article by Karl Radek (Parabellum), "Annexations and Social-Democracy," in *Berner Tagwacht* (*Berne Guardian*), Nos. 252, 253, Oct. 28-29, 1915.—*Ed.*

where this movement is a thing not of the past, but of the present and the future. Suffice it to mention India, China, Persia, Egypt. Imperialism, further, means that capital has outgrown the framework of national states; it means the widening and sharpening of national oppression on a new historical basis. It follows from this, in contradiction to the conception of Comrade Parabellum, that we must *connect* the revolutionary struggle for socialism with a revolutionary program on the national question.

As to Comrade Parabellum, he, in the name of a socialist revolution, scornfully rejects a consistently revolutionary program in the realm of democracy. This is incorrect. The proletariat cannot become victor save through democracy, *i.e.,* through introducing complete democracy and through combining with every step of its movement democratic demands formulated most vigorously, most decisively. It is senseless to *contrast* the socialist revolution and the revolutionary struggle against capitalism to *one* of the questions of democracy, in this case the national question. On the contrary, we must combine the revolutionary struggle against capitalism with a revolutionary program and revolutionary tactics relative to *all* democratic demands: a republic, a militia, officials elected by the people, equal rights for women, self-determination of nations, etc. While capitalism exists, all these demands are realizable only as an exception, and in an incomplete, distorted form. Basing ourselves on democracy as it already exists, exposing its incompleteness under capitalism, we advocate the overthrow of capitalism, expropriation of the bourgeoisie as a necessary basis both for the abolition of the poverty of the masses and for a complete and manifold realization of all democratic reforms. Some of those reforms will be started prior to the overthrow of the bourgeoisie, others in the process of the overthrow, still others after it has been accomplished. The socialist revolution is by no means a single battle; on the contrary, it is an epoch of a whole series of battles around *all* problems of economic and democratic reforms, which can be completed only by the expropriation of the bourgeoisie. It is for the sake of this final aim that we must formulate in a consistently revolutionary manner every one of our democratic demands. It is quite conceivable that the workers of a certain country may overthrow the bourgeoisie *before* even one fundamental democratic reform has been realized in full. It is entirely inconceivable, however, that the proletariat as an historical class will be able to defeat the bourgeoisie if it is not prepared for this task by being educated in the spirit of the most consistent and determined revolutionary democracy.

Imperialism is the progressing oppression of the nations of the world by a handful of great powers; it is an epoch of wars among them for the widening and strengthening of national oppression; it is the epoch when the masses of the people are deceived by the hypocritical social-patriots, *i.e.*, people who under the pretext of "freedom of nations," "right of nations to self-determination," and "defense of the fatherland" justify and defend the oppression of a majority of the world's nations by the great powers.

This is just why the central point in a program of Social-Democrats must be that distinction between oppressing and oppressed nations, since the distinction is the *essence* of imperialism, and is fraudulently evaded by the social-patriots, Kautsky included. This distinction is not important from the point of view of bourgeois pacifism, or the petty-bourgeois utopia of peaceful competition between independent nations under capitalism, but it is most important from the point of view of the revolutionary struggle against imperialism. From this distinction there follows *our* consistently democratic and revolutionary definition of the "right of nations to self-determination," which is in accord with the general task of the immediate struggle for socialism. It is in the name of this right, and fighting for its unequivocal recognition, that the Social-Democrats of the *oppressing* nations must demand the freedom of separation for the oppressed nations, for otherwise recognition of the equal rights of nations and international solidarity of the workers in reality remains an empty phrase, a hypocritical gesture. The Social-Democrats of the *oppressed* nations, however, must view as foremost the demand for the unity and the *fusion* of the workers of the oppressed nations with the workers of the oppressing nations, because otherwise those Social-Democrats involuntarily become the allies of one or the other national bourgeoisie, which *always* betrays the interest of the people and of democracy, and which in its turn is *always* ready for annexations and for oppressing other nations.

The approach to the national problem by the end of the sixties of the nineteenth century may serve as an instructive example. The petty-bourgeois democrats, devoid of every idea concerning the class struggle and the socialist revolution, pictured a utopia of peaceful competition between free and equal nations under capitalism. The Proudhonists "denied" entirely the national question and the right of self-determination of nations and precisely from the point of view of the immediate tasks of a social revolution. Marx scoffed at Proudhonism showing its affinity to chauvinism ("All Europe must sit quietly and obediently on its behind until the masters abolish 'poverty and ignorance' in France";[11] "by the denial of the national question, they seem to understand, without being aware of it, the swallowing up of the nations by the exemplary French nation").[12] Marx demanded the *separation of Ireland* from England, "although after the separation there may come federation,"[13] and not from the standpoint of the petty-bourgeois utopia of a peaceful capitalism, not from considerations of "justice to Ireland," but from the standpoint of the interests of the revolutionary struggle of the proletariat of the *oppressing, i.e., the English, nation* against capitalism. The freedom of *that* nation was cramped and mutilated by the fact that it oppressed another nation. The internationalism of the *English* proletariat would have remained a hypocritical phrase were *it* not to demand the separation of Ireland. Marx never was in favor of small states, or of splitting up states, or of the federation principle. Still he considered the separation of an oppressed nation as a step towards federation, consequently not towards a splitting of nations but towards concentration, towards political and economic concentration, but concentration on the basis of democracy. From Comrade Parabellum's standpoint, Marx must have fought an "illusory" battle when he demanded the separation of Ireland. In reality, however, only this demand was a consistent revolutionary program, only it corresponded to internationalism, only it represented concentration *not* along the lines of imperialism.

The imperialism of our days has brought about a situation where the oppression of nations by the great powers is a common phenomenon. It is precisely the standpoint of struggle against the social-patriots of the great-power nations that are now waging an imperialist war for the purpose of strengthening the oppression of nations—that are oppressing the majority of nations of the world and the majority of the earth's population—it is precisely this standpoint that must become the decisive, cardinal, basic point in the Social-Democratic national program.

Let us now cast a glance at the present-day currents of Social-Democratic thought on this question. The petty-bourgeois utopians who dream of equality and peace among nations under capitalism have ceded their place to the social-patriots. In battling against the former, Comrade Parabellum battles against windmills, thereby unwillingly aiding the latter. What, then, is the program of the social-patriots on the national question?

They either entirely deny the right to self-determination, using arguments like those of Comrade Parabellum (Cunow, Parvus, the Russian opportunists Semkovsky, Liebman, etc.), or they recognize that right in an obviously hypocritical fashion, namely, without applying it to precisely those nations which are oppressed by their own nation or by the military allies of their own nation (Plekhanov, Hyndman, all the Francophile social-patriots, Scheidemann and Co., etc.). It is Kautsky, however, that gives the formulation of the social-patriot lie that is most plausible and therefore most dangerous for the proletariat. In words he is *for* self-determination of nations; in words he says that the Social-Democratic Party *"die Selbstständigkeit der Nationen allseitig* [!!] *und rückhaltlos* [??] *[risum tenatis, amici!] achtet und fordert"* * [*Neue Zeit*, 33, II, p. 241, May 21, 1915]. In reality, however, he adapts the national program to the prevailing social-patriotism; he distorts and mutilates it without clearly determining the duties of the Socialists of the oppressing nations, and he even falsifies the democratic principle itself when he says that to demand "state independence" (*staatliche Selbstständigkeit*) for every nation would mean to demand *"too much"* (*zu viel*) (*Neue Zeit*, 33, II, p. 77, May 16, 1915). "National autonomy" alone, according to his sagacious opinion, is sufficient. Kautsky thus evades the most important question which the imperialist bourgeoisie does not allow one to touch upon, namely, the question of the *boundaries of a state* which rests on the oppression of nations. Kautsky, to please the bourgeoisie, throws out of the national program of the Social-Democratic Party the most essential thing. The bourgeoisie will promise any "national autonomy," if only the proletariat remains within the framework of legality and peacefully submits to the bourgeoisie on the question of the state boundaries. Kautsky formulates the national program of Social-Democracy not like a revolutionary but like a reformist.

Comrade Parabellum's national program or, more correctly, his assurances to the effect that "we are against annexations" is eagerly subscribed to by the German *Parteivorstand*,† Kautsky, Plekhanov and Co. just because that program does not expose the dominating social-patriots. Bourgeois pacifists would also be willing to sign this program. Parabellum's splendid general program ("revolutionary mass struggle against capitalism") serves him, as it did the Proudhonists of the 'sixties, not to work out an uncompromising, equally revolutionary program on the national question in conformity with the general program and its spirit, but only to clear the field for the social-patriots! The majority of

* "Respect and demand everywhere [!!] and without reservations [??] [withhold your laughter, friends!] the independence of nations."—*Ed.*
† Central Committee of the German Social-Democratic Party.—*Ed.*

70

the Socialists of the world belong, in our imperialist epoch, to nations that oppress other nations and strive to widen the scope of that oppression. This is why our "struggle against annexations" will be meaningless and not at all terrifying to the social-patriots, if we do not declare that a Socialist of an oppressing nation who does not conduct a propaganda, both in peace and war time, in favor of *separation,* a Socialist of an oppressing nation who does not conduct such a propaganda, in *defiance* of the governmental prohibitions, *i.e.,* in a free, *i.e.,* in an illegal press, is not a Socialist or an internationalist but a chauvinist, whose adherence to national equality is sheer hypocrisy.

About Russia, which has not yet completed its bourgeois-democratic revolution, Comrade Parabellum says only one sentence:

"Selbst das wirtschaftlich sehr zurückgebliebene Russland hat in der Haltung der polnischen, lettischen, armenischen Bourgeoisie gezeigt, dass nicht nur die militärische Bewachung es ist, die die Völker in diesem "Zuchthaus der Völker" zusammenhält, sondern Bedürfnisse der kapitalistischen Expansion, für die das ungeheure Territorium ein glänzender Boden der Entwicklung ist."

This is not a "Social-Democratic," but a liberal-bourgeois point of view, not an internationalist but a Great-Russian chauvinist point of view. It is unfortunate that Comrade Parabellum, who so excellently fights the German social-patriots, evidently has very little acquaintance with Russian chauvinism! To make a Social-Democratic sentence and to allow Social-Democratic conclusions to be drawn from the above sentence of Comrade Parabellum, it must be changed and amended in the following way:

Russia *is* a prison of peoples not only because of the military, feudal character of tsarism, not only because the Great Russian bourgeoisie supports tsarism, but also because the Polish, Lettish, etc., bourgeoisie has sacrificed the freedom of nations and democracy in general for the interests of capitalist expansion. The proletariat of Russia, marching at the head of the people, cannot complete the victorious democratic revolution (which is its immediate task); neither can it fight together with its brothers, the proletarians of Europe, for a social revolution, without demanding at once full and *"unreserved"* freedom of separation from Russia for all the

* "Even the economically very backward Russia proved in the stand taken by the Polish, Lettish, Armenian bourgeoisie that it is not only military supervision that keeps the peoples in that 'prison of peoples' together, but also the need for capitalist expansion, for which the vast territory is a splendid ground for development."—*Ed.*

71

nations oppressed by Russia. This we demand not as something independent from our revolutionary struggle for socialism, but because this struggle would remain an idle phrase if it were not linked with a revolutionary approach to all the questions of democracy, including the national question. We demand the freedom of self-determination, *i.e.,* independence, *i.e.,* the freedom of separation for the oppressed nations, not because we dream of an economically atomized world, nor because we cherish the ideal of small states, but on the contrary because we are for large states and for a coming closer, even a fusion of nations, but on a truly democratic, truly internationalist basis, which is *unthinkable* without the freedom of separation. In the same way as Marx in 1869 demanded the separation of Ireland, not for the purpose of splitting England, but for a subsequent free alliance of Ireland with England, not for the sake of "justice to Ireland," but for the interests of the revolutionary struggle of the *English* proletariat, so we at present consider the refusal by the Socialists of Russia to demand freedom of self-determination for the nations, in the sense indicated by us above, as a direct betrayal of democracy, internationalism, and socialism.

Written November, 1915, in German.

Collected Works, Vol. XVIII, pp. 367-73.

The Socialist Revolution and the Right of Nations to Self-Determination (Theses)

1. IMPERIALISM, SOCIALISM, AND THE LIBERATION OF OPPRESSED NATIONS

Imperialism is the highest stage of development of capitalism. Capital in the advanced countries has outgrown the boundaries of national states. It has established monopoly in place of competition, thus creating all the objective prerequisites for the achievement of socialism. Hence, in Western Europe and in the United States of America, the revolutionary struggle of the proletariat for the overthrow of the capitalist governments, for the expropriation of the bourgeoisie, is on the order of the day. Imperialism is forcing the masses into this struggle by sharpening class antagonisms to an immense degree, by worsening the conditions of the masses both economically—trusts and the high cost of living, and politically—growth of militarism, frequent wars, increase of reaction, strengthening and extension of national oppression and colonial plunder. Victorious socialism must achieve complete democracy and, consequently, not only bring about the complete equality of nations, but also give effect to the right of oppressed nations to self-determination, *i.e.,* the right to free political secession. Socialist parties which fail to prove by all their activities now, as well as during the revolution and after its victory, that they will free the enslaved nations and establish relations with them on the basis of a free union—and a free union is a lying phrase without right to secession—such parties would be committing treachery to socialism.

Of course, democracy is also a form of state which must disappear when the state disappears, but this will take place only in the process of transition from completely victorious and consolidated socialism to complete communism.

2. THE SOCIALIST REVOLUTION
AND THE STRUGGLE FOR DEMOCRACY

The socialist revolution is not one single act, not one single battle on a single front, but a whole epoch of intensified class conflicts, a long series of battles on all fronts, *i.e.*, battles around all the problems of economics and politics, which can culminate only in the expropriation of the bourgeoisie. It would be a ˙fundamental mistake to suppose that the struggle for democracy can divert the proletariat from the socialist revolution, or obscure, or overshadow it, etc. On the contrary, just as socialism cannot be victorious unless it introduces complete democracy, so the proletariat will be unable to prepare for victory over the bourgeoisie unless it wages a many-sided, consistent, and revolutionary struggle for democracy.

It would be no less mistaken to delete any of the points of the democratic program, for example, the point of self-determination of nations, on the ground that it is "infeasible," or that it is "illusory" under imperialism. The assertion that the right of nations to self-determination cannot be achieved within the framework of capitalism may be understood either in its absolute, economic sense, or in the conventional, political sense.

In the first case, the assertion is fundamentally wrong in theory. First, in this sense, it is impossible to achieve such things as labor money, or the abolition of crises, etc., under capitalism. But it is entirely incorrect to argue that the self-determination of nations is *likewise* infeasible. Second, even the one example of the secession of Norway from Sweden in 1905 is sufficient to refute the argument that it is "infeasible" in this sense. Third, it would be ridiculous to deny that, with a slight change in political and strategical relationships, for example, between Germany and England, the formation of new states, Polish, Indian, etc., would be quite "feasible" very soon. Fourth, finance capital, in its striving towards expansion, will "freely" buy and bribe the freest, most democratic and republican government and the elected officials of any country, however "independent" it may be. The domination of finance capital, as of capital in general, cannot be abolished by *any* kind of reforms in the realm of political democracy, and self-determination belongs wholly and exclusively to this realm. The domination of finance capital, however, does not in the least destroy the significance of political democracy as the freer, wider, and more distinct *form* of class oppression and class struggle. Hence, all arguments about the "impossibility of achieving" economically one of the demands of

74

political democracy under capitalism reduce themselves to a theoretically incorrect definition of the general and fundamental relations of capitalism and of political democracy in general.

In the second case, this assertion is incomplete and inaccurate, for not only the right of nations to self-determination, but *all* the fundamental demands of political democracy are "possible of achievement" under imperialism, only in an incomplete, in a mutilated form and as a rare exception (for example, the secession of Norway from Sweden in 1905). The demand for the immediate liberation of the colonies, as advanced by all revolutionary Social-Democrats, is also "impossible of achievement" under capitalism without a series of revolutions. This does not imply, however, that Social-Democracy must refrain from conducting an immediate and most determined struggle for *all* these demands—to refrain would merely be to the advantage of the bourgeoisie and reaction. On the contrary, it implies that it is necessary to formulate and put forward all these demands, not in a reformist, but in a revolutionary way; not by keeping within the framework of bourgeois legality, but by breaking through it; not by confining oneself to parliamentary speeches and verbal protests, but by drawing the masses into real action, by widening and fomenting the struggle for every kind of fundamental, democratic demand, right up to and including the direct onslaught of the proletariat against the bourgeoisie, *i.e.,* to the socialist revolution, which will expropriate the bourgeoisie. The socialist revolution may break out not only in consequence of a great strike, a street demonstration, a hunger riot, a mutiny in the forces, or a colonial rebellion, but also in consequence of any political crisis, like the Dreyfus affair, the Zabern incident,* or in connection with a referendum on the secession of an oppressed nation, etc.

The intensification of national oppression under imperialism makes it necessary for Social-Democracy not to renounce what the bourgeoisie describes as the "utopian" struggle for the freedom of

* The Zabern incident was the conflict which arose in 1913 as a result of the chauvinist, high-handed treatment of the inhabitants of Zabern (Alsace-Lorraine) by a German officer, Lieutenant Forstner. When the indignant population attempted to voice their protest openly, Forstner, with the approval of the higher military authorities and even of Bethmann-Hollweg, the Chancellor, proclaimed martial law in the town and terrorized the inhabitants. Owing to mass pressure the incident was discussed in the Reichstag. Forstner was championed by the Chancellor and the Minister of War, but the overwhelming majority of the members (293 as against 54) expressed their condemnation by passing a vote of censure on the Chancellor.—*Ed.*

nations to secede, but, on the contrary, to take more advantage than ever before of conflicts arising *also* on this ground for the purpose of rousing mass action and revolutionary attacks upon the bourgeoisie.

3. THE MEANING OF THE RIGHT TO SELF-DETERMINATION AND ITS RELATION TO FEDERATION

The right of nations to self-determination means only the right to independence in a political sense, the right to free, political secession from the oppressing nation. Concretely, this political, democratic demand implies complete freedom to carry on agitation in favor of secession, and freedom to settle the question of secession by means of a referendum of the nation that desires to secede. Consequently, this demand is by no means identical with the demand for secession, for partition, for the formation of small states. It is merely the logical expression of the struggle against national oppression in every form. The more closely the democratic system of state approximates to complete freedom of secession, the rarer and weaker will the striving for secession be in practice; for the advantages of large states, both from the point of view of economic progress and from the point of view of the interests of the masses, are beyond doubt, and these advantages increase with the growth of capitalism. The recognition of self-determination is not the same as making federation a principle. One may be a determined opponent of this principle and a partisan of democratic centralism and yet prefer federation to national inequality as the only path towards complete democratic centralism. It was precisely from this point of view that Marx, although a centralist, preferred even the federation of Ireland with England to the forcible subjection of Ireland to the English.[14]

The aim of socialism is not only to abolish the present division of mankind into small states and all national isolation; not only to bring the nations closer to each other, but also to merge them. And in order to achieve this aim, we must, on the one hand, explain to the masses the reactionary nature of the ideas of Renner and O. Bauer concerning so-called "cultural national autonomy" and, on the other hand, demand the liberation of the oppressed nations, not only in general, nebulous phrases, not in empty declamations, not by "postponing" the question until socialism is established, but in a clearly and precisely formulated political program which

76

shall particularly take into account the hypocrisy and cowardice of the Socialists in the oppressing nations. Just as mankind can achieve the abolition of classes only by passing through the transition period of the dictatorship of the oppressed class, so mankind can achieve the inevitable merging of nations only by passing through the transition period of complete liberation of all the oppressed nations, *i.e.,* their freedom to secede.

4. THE PROLETARIAN-REVOLUTIONARY PRESENTATION OF THE QUESTION OF THE SELF-DETERMINATION OF NATIONS

Not only the demand for the self-determination of nations but *all* the items of our democratic minimum program were advanced *before us,* as far back as as the seventeenth and eighteenth centuries, by the petty bourgeoisie. And the petty bourgeoisie, believing in "peaceful" capitalism, continues to this day to advance *all* these demands in a utopian way, without seeing the class sruggle and the fact that it has become intensified under democracy. The idea of a peaceful union of equal nations under imperialism, which deceives the people, and which the Kautskyists advocate, is precisely of this nature. As against this philistine, opportunist utopia, the program of Social-Democracy must point out that under imperialism the division of nations into oppressing and oppressed ones is a fundamental, most important and inevitable fact.

The proletariat of the oppressing nations cannot confine itself to the general hackneyed phrases against annexations and for the equal rights of nations in general, that may be repeated by any pacifist bourgeois. The proletariat cannot evade the question that is particularly "unpleasant" for the imperialist bourgeoisie, namely, the question of the *frontiers* of a state that is based on national oppression. The proletariat cannot but fight against the forcible retention of the oppressed nations within the boundaries of a given state, and this is exactly what the struggle for the right of self-determination means. The proletariat must demand the right of political secession for the colonies and for the nations that "its own" nation oppresses. Unless it does this, proletarian internationalism will remain a meaningless phrase; mutual confidence and class solidarity between the workers of the oppressing and oppressed nations will be impossible; the hypocrisy of the reformist and Kautskyan advocates of self-determination who maintain silence about the nations which are oppressed by "their" nation and forcibly retained within "their" state will remain unexposed.

The Socialists of the oppressed nations, on the other hand, must particularly fight for and maintain complete, absolute unity (also organizational) between the workers of the oppressed nation and the workers of the oppressing nation. Without such unity it will be impossible to maintain an independent proletarian policy and class solidarity with the proletariat of other countries in the face of all the subterfuge, treachery, and trickery of the bourgeoisie; for the bourgeoisie of the oppressed nations always converts the slogan of national liberation into a means for deceiving the workers; in internal politics it utilizes these slogans as a means for concluding reactionary agreements with the bourgeoisie of the ruling nation (for instance, the Poles in Austria and Russia, who entered into pacts with reaction in order to oppress the Jews and the Ukrainians); in the realm of foreign politics it strives to enter into pacts with one of the rival imperialist powers for the purpose of achieving its own predatory aims (the policies of the small states in the Balkans, etc.).

The fact that the struggle for national liberation against one imperialist power may, under certain circumstances, be utilized by another "Great" Power in its equally imperialist interests should have no more weight in inducing Social-Democracy to renounce its recognition of the right of nations to self-determination than the numerous cases of the bourgeoisie utilizing republican slogans for the purpose of political deception and financial robbery, for example, in the Latin countries, have had in inducing them to renounce republicanism.*

* Needless to say, to repudiate the right of self-determination on the ground that logically it means "defense of the fatherland" would be quite ridiculous. With equal logic, *i.e.*, with equal shallowness, the social-chauvinists of 1914-16 apply this argument to every one of the demands of democracy (for instance, to republicanism), and to every formulation of the struggle against national oppression, in order to justify "defense of the fatherland." Marxism arrives at the recognition of defense of the fatherland, for example, in the wars of the Great French Revolution and the Garibaldi wars in Europe, and at the repudiation of defense of the fatherland in the imperialist war of 1914-16, from the analysis of the specific historical circumstances of each separate war, and not from some "general principle," or some separate item of a program.

5. MARXISM AND PROUDHONISM
ON THE NATIONAL QUESTION

In contrast to the petty-bourgeois democrats, Marx regarded all democratic demands without exception not as an absolute, but as a historical expression of the struggle of the masses of the people, led by the bourgeoisie, against feudalism. There is not a single democratic demand which could not serve, and has not served, under certain conditions, as an instrument of the bourgeoisie for deceiving the workers. To single out one of the demands of political democracy, namely, the self-determination of nations, and to oppose it to all the rest, is fundamentally wrong in theory. In practice, the proletariat will be able to retain its independence only if it subordinates its struggle for all the democratic demands, not excluding the demand for a republic, to its revolutionary struggle for the overthrow of the bourgeoisie.

On the other hand, in contrast to the Proudhonists, who "repudiated" the national problem "in the name of the social revolution," Marx, having in mind mainly the interests of the proletarian class struggle in the advanced countries, put into the forefront the fundamental principle of internationalism and socialism, *viz.*, that no nation can be free if it oppresses other nations. It was precisely from the standpoint of the interests of the revolutionary movement of the German workers that Marx in 1848 demanded that victorious democracy in Germany should proclaim and grant freedom to the nations that the Germans were oppressing. It was precisely from the standpoint of the revolutionary struggle of the English workers that Marx in 1869 demanded the separation of Ireland from England, and added: "although after the separation there may come federation." Only by putting forward this demand did Marx really educate the English workers in the spirit of internationalism. Only in this way was he able to oppose the revolutionary solution of a given historical problem to the opportunists and bourgeois reformism, which even now, half a century later, has failed to achieve the Irish "reform." Only in this way was Marx able—unlike the apologists of capital who shout about the right of small nations to secession being utopian and impossible, and about the progressive nature not only of economic but also of political concentration—to urge the progressive nature of this concentration in a *non*-imperialist manner, to urge the bringing together of the nations, not by force, but on the basis of a free union of the proletarians of all countries. Only in this way was Marx able, *also* in the sphere of the solution of national problems, to oppose the revolutionary action of the masses to verbal and often hypocritical recognition of the equality and the self-determination of nations. The imperialist war of 1914-16 and the Augean stables of hypocrisy of the opportunists and Kautskyists it exposed have strikingly confirmed the correctness of Marx's policy, which must serve as the model for all the advanced countries; for all of them now oppress other nations.*

6. THREE TYPES OF COUNTRIES IN RELATION TO SELF-DETERMINATION OF NATIONS

In this respect, countries must be divided into three main types:

First, the advanced capitalist countries of Western Europe and the United States of America. In these countries the bourgeois, progressive, national movements came to an end long ago. Every one of these "great" nations oppresses other nations in the colonies and within its own country. The tasks of the proletariat of these ruling nations are the same as those of the proletariat in England in the nineteenth century in relation to Ireland.†

*Reference is often made—recently, for instance, by the German chauvinist Lensch, in *Die Glocke,* No. 8-9—to the fact that Marx's adverse attitude to the national movement of certain peoples, for example, the Czechs in 1848, refutes the necessity of recognizing the self-determination of nations from the point of view of Marxism. This is incorrect, for in 1848 there were historical and political grounds for drawing a distinction between "reactionary" and revolutionary democratic nations. Marx was right when he condemned the former and defended the latter. The right to self-determination is one of the demands of democracy which must naturally be subordinated to the general interests of democracy. In 1848 and subsequent years, those general interests were concentrated primarily in the struggle against tsarism.

† In some small states which have remained out of the war of 1914-1916, for example, Holland and Switzerland, the bourgeoisie strongly urges the slogan "self-determination of nations" to justify participation in the imperialist war. This is one of the motives that induces the Social-Democrats in such countries to repudiate self-determination. In this case the correct proletarian policy, namely, the repudiation of "defense of the fatherland" in an *imperialist* war is defended by wrong arguments. What results is a distortion of Marxian theory, while in practice we have a peculiar small-nation narrow-mindedness, which forgets about the *hundreds of millions* of the population of nations that are enslaved by the "Great Power" nations. Comrade Gorter, in his excellent pamphlet *Imperialism, the War and Social-Democracy,* wrongly rejects the principle of self-determination of nations, but correctly *applies* it when he demands the *immediate* granting of "political and *national* independence" to the Dutch Indies and exposes the Dutch opportunists who refuse to put forward this demand and to fight for it.

80

Second, Eastern Europe: Austria, the Balkans and particularly Russia. Here it was the twentieth century that particularly developed the bourgeois-democratic national movements and intensified the national struggle. The tasks of the proletariat in these countries —in regard to the consummation of their bourgeois-democratic reformation, as well as in regard to assisting the socialist revolution in other countries—cannot be achieved unless it champions the right of nations to self-determination. In this connection the most difficult but most important task is to merge the class struggle of the workers in the oppressing nations with the class struggle of the workers in the oppressed nations.

Third, the semi-colonial countries, like China, Persia, Turkey, and all the colonies, which have a combined population amounting to a billion. In these countries the bourgeois-democratic movements have either hardly begun, or are far from having been completed. Socialists must not only demand the unconditional and immediate liberation of the colonies without compensation—and this demand in its political expression signifies nothing more nor less than the recognition of the right to self-determination—but must render determined support to the more revolutionary elements in the bourgeois-democratic movements for national liberation in these countries and assist their rebellion—and if need be, their revolutionary war—*against* the imperialist powers that oppress them.

7. SOCIAL-CHAUVINISM AND SELF-DETERMINATION OF NATIONS

The imperialist epoch and the war of 1914-16 have particularly brought to the forefront the task of fighting against chauvinism and nationalism in the advanced countries. On the question of the self-determination of nations, there are two main shades of opinion among the social-chauvinists, *i.e.*, the opportunists and the Kautskyists, who embellish the reactionary, imperialist war by declaring it to be a war in "defense of the fatherland."

On the one hand, we see the rather avowed servants of the bourgeoisie who defend annexations on the ground that imperialism and political concentration are progressive and who repudiate the right to self-determination on the ground that it is utopian, illusory, petty-bourgeois, etc. Among these may be included Cunow, Parvus, and the extreme opportunists in Germany, a section of the Fabians and the trade union leaders in England, and the opportunists, Semkovsky, Liebman, Yurkevich, etc., in Russia.

On the other hand, we see the Kautskyists, including Vandervelde, Renaudel, and many of the pacifists in England, France, etc. These stand for unity with the first-mentioned group, and in practice their conduct is the same in that they advocate the right to self-determination in a purely verbal and hypocritical way. They regard the demand for the freedom of political secession as being "excessive" (*"zu viel velangt"*—Kautsky, in the *Neue Zeit*, May 21, 1915); they do not advocate the need for revolutionary tactics, especially for the Socialists in the oppressing nations, but, on the contrary, they gloss over their revolutionary duties, they justify their opportunism, they make it easier to deceive the people, they evade precisely the question of the *frontiers* of a state which forcibly retains subject nations, etc.

Both groups are opportunists who prostitute Marxism and who have lost all capacity to understand the theoretical significance and the practical urgency of Marx's tactics, an example of which he gave in relation to Ireland.

The specific question of annexations has become a particularly urgent one owing to the war. But what is annexation? Clearly, to protest against annexations implies either the recognition of the right of self-determination of nations, or that the protest is based on a pacifist phrase which defends the *status quo* and opposes *all* violence including revolutionary violence. Such a phrase is radically wrong, and incompatible with Marxism.

8. THE CONCRETE TASKS OF THE PROLETARIAT IN THE IMMEDIATE FUTURE

The socialist revolution may begin in the very near future. In that event the proletariat will be faced with the immediate task of capturing power, of expropriating the banks, and of introducing other dictatorial measures. In such a situation, the bourgeoisie, and particularly intellectuals like the Fabians and the Kautskyists, will strive to disrupt and to hinder the revolution, to restrict it to limited democratic aims. While *all* purely democratic demands may—at a time when the proletarians have already begun to storm the bulwarks of bourgeois power—serve, in a certain sense, as a hindrance to the revolution, nevertheless, the necessity of proclaiming and granting freedom to *all* oppressed nations (*i.e.,* their right to self-determination) will be as urgent in the socialist revolution as it was urgent for the victory of the bourgeois-democratic revolution, for example, in Germany in 1848, or in Russia in 1905.

However, five, ten, and even more years may pass before the socialist revolution begins. In that case, the task will be to educate the masses in a revolutionary spirit so as to make it impossible for Socialist chauvinists and opportunists to belong to the workers' party and to achieve a victory similar to that of 1914-16. It will be the duty of the Socialists to explain to the masses that English Socialists who fail to demand the freedom of secession for the colonies and for Ireland; that German Socialists who fail to demand the freedom of secession for the colonies, for the Alsatians, for the Danes, and for the Poles, and who fail to carry direct revolutionary propaganda and revolutionary mass action to the field of struggle against national oppression, who fail to take advantage of cases like the Zabern incident to conduct widespread underground propaganda among the proletariat of the oppressing nation, to organize street demonstrations and revolutionary mass actions; that Russian Socialists who fail to demand freedom of secession for Finland, Poland, the Ukraine, etc., etc.—are behaving like chauvinists, like lackeys of the blood-and-mud-stained imperialist monarchies and the imperialist bourgeoisie.

9. THE ATTITUDE OF RUSSIAN AND POLISH SOCIAL-DEMOCRACY AND OF THE SECOND INTERNATIONAL TO SELF-DETERMINATION

The difference between the revolutionary Social-Democrats of Russia and the Polish Social-Democrats on the question of self-determination came to the surface as early as 1903 at the congress which adopted the program of the Russian Social-Democratic Labor Party, and which, despite the protest of the Polish Social-Democratic delegation, inserted into that program point 9, which recognizes the right of nations to self-determination. Since then the Polish Social-Democrats have never repeated, in the name of their party, the proposal to delete point 9 from our program, or to substitute some other formulation for it.

In Russia—where no less than 57 per cent, *i.e.,* over 100,000,000 of the population, belong to oppressed nations, where those nations mainly inhabit the border provinces, where some of those nations are more cultured than the Great Russians, where the political system is distinguished by its particularly barbarous and medieval character, where the bourgeois-democratic revolution has not yet been completed—the recognition of the right of the nations oppressed by tsarism to free secession from Russia is absolutely obligatory for Social-Democracy in the interests of its democratic and socialist tasks. Our party, which was re-established in January 1912,* adopted a resolution in 1913[15] reiterating the right to self-determination and explaining it in the concrete sense outlined above. The orgy of Great-Russian chauvinism raging in 1914-16 among the bourgeoisie and the opportunist Socialists (Rubanovich, Plekhanov, *Nashe Dyelo,* etc.) prompts us to insist on this demand more strongly than ever and to declare that those who reject it serve, in practice, as a bulwark of Great-Russian chauvinism and tsarism. Our party declares that it emphatically repudiates all responsibility for such opposition to the right of self-determination.

The latest formulation of the position of Polish Social-Democracy on the national question (the declaration made by Polish Social-Democracy at the Zimmerwald Conference) contains the following ideas: This declaration condemns the German and other governments which regard the "Polish provinces" as a hostage in the forthcoming game of compensations and thus *"deprive the Polish people of the opportunity to decide its own fate."* The declaration says: "Polish Social-Democracy emphatically and solemnly protests against the *recarving and partition of a whole country. . . ."* It condemns the Socialists who left to the Hohenzollerns "the task of *liberating the oppressed nations."* It expresses the conviction that only participation in the impending struggle of the revolutionary international proletariat, in the struggle for socialism, *"will break the fetters of national oppression* and abolish *all forms of foreign* domination, and secure for *the Polish people* the possibility of all-sided, free development as an *equal* member in a League of Nations." The declaration also recognizes the present war to be *"doubly* fratricidal" *"for the Poles."* (Bulletin of the International Socialist Committee, No. 2, September 27, 1915, p. 15.)

There is no difference in substance between these postulates and the recognition of the right of nations to self-determination except that their political formulation is still more diffuse and vague than the majority of the programs and resolutions of the Second International. Any attempt to express these ideas in precise political formulae and to determine whether they apply to the capitalist system or only to the socialist system will prove still more strikingly

* The Bolshevik Conference at Prague.—*Ed.*

the error committed by the Polish Social-Democrats in repudiating the self-determination of nations.

The decision of the International Socialist Congress held in London in 1896, which recognized the self-determination of nations, must, on the basis of the above-mentioned postulates, be supplemented by references to: (1) the particular urgency of this demand under imperialism; (2) the politically conditional nature and the class content of all the demands of political democracy, including this demand; (3) the necessity of drawing a distinction between the concrete tasks of the Social-Democrats in the oppressing nations and those in oppressed nations; (4) the inconsistent, purely verbal, and, therefore, as far as its political significance is concerned, hypocritical recognition of self-determination by the opportunists and Kautskyists; (5) the actual identity of the chauvinists and those Social-Democrats, particularly the Social-Democrats of the Great Powers (Great Russians, Anglo-Americans, Germans, French, Italians, Japanese, etc.), who fail to champion the freedom of secession for the colonies and nations oppressed by "their own" nations; (6) the necessity of subordinating the struggle for this demand, as well as for all the fundamental demands of political democracy, to the immediate revolutionary mass struggle for the overthrow of the bourgeois governments and for the achievement of socialism.

To transplant to the International the point of view of some of the small nations—particularly the point of view of the Polish Social-Democrats, who, in their struggle against the Polish bourgeoisie which is deceiving the people with nationalist slogans, were misled into repudiating self-determination—would be a theoretical error. It would be the substitution of Proudhonism for Marxism and, in practice, would result in rendering involuntary support to the most dangerous chauvinism and opportunism of the Great Power nations.

Editorial Board of *Sotsial-Demokrat,* central organ of the R.S.D.L.P.

Postscript. In the latest issue of the *Neue Zeit,* dated March 3, 1916, Kautsky openly extends a Christian hand of reconciliation to the representative of the filthiest German chauvinism, Austerlitz. He rejects the freedom of secession for the nations oppressed by the Austria of the Hapsburgs, but accepts it for *Russian* Poland, thus rendering lackey's service to Hindenburg and Wilhelm II. A better self-exposure of Kautskyism could not be desired!

Written in the beginning of March, 1916.

Collected Works, Vol. XIX, pp. 47-60.

The Discussion on Self-Determination

Summed Up

In No. 2 of the Marxist magazine of the Zimmerwald Left, the *Predvestnik* (*Vorbote*, No. 2, April 1916) there appeared theses for and against self-determination of nations, signed by the editors of our central organ, the *Sotsial-Demokrat,* and by the editors of the organ of the Polish Social-Democratic opposition, *Gazeta Robotnicza.* The reader will find above [16] a reproduction of the former and a translation of the latter theses. This, perhaps, is the first time that this question has been raised so broadly in the international arena; the discussion which was conducted in the German Marxist magazine, *Neue Zeit,* twenty years ago, 1895-96, before the London International Socialist Congress of 1896, by Rosa Luxemburg, K. Kautsky, and the Polish *Nepodleglostsevtsi* (advocates of Polish independence, the P.P.S.), representing three different points of view, revolved only around Poland. As far as we know, the question of self-determination has up to now been discussed more or less systematically only by the Dutch and the Poles. Let us hope that the *Vorbote* will stimulate a discussion of this now very urgent question among the English, Americans, French, Germans, and Italians. Official socialism, represented by open partisans of "their" respective governments, Plekhanov, David and Co., as well as by the covert defenders of opportunism, the Kautskyists (including Axelrod, Martov, Chkheidze, etc.), has spun such a web of lies around this question that for a long time there will inevitably be, on the one hand, efforts to wriggle and avoid discussion, and on the other hand, demands from the workers for "direct answers" to "vexed questions." We shall endeavor to keep our readers informed about the conflict of opinion among foreign Socialists.

For us, Russian Social-Democrats, however, the question is of particular importance. This discussion is a continuation of the one of 1903 and 1913; since the war this question has caused some wavering of opinion among members of our party; it has been made acute by the cunning attempts of eminent leaders of the Gvozdevist, or chauvinist labor party, such as Martov and Chkheidze, to evade the main issue. It is therefore necessary to give at least a preliminary summation of the discussion which has already begun in the international arena.

As is evident from the theses, our Polish comrades give us a direct answer to some of our arguments, for instance, on Marxism and Proudhonism. For the most part, however, they reply to us, not directly, but indirectly, by advancing *their own* statements. Let us examine their direct and indirect answers.

SOCIALISM AND THE SELF-DETERMINATION OF NATIONS

We maintained that it would be a betrayal of socialism to refuse to grant the right of self-determination of nations under socialism. To this the reply is made: "The right of self-determination is not applicable to socialist society." The disagreement is fundamental. What is its source?

"We know," our opponents contend, "that socialism will eliminate all national oppression because it will eliminate all class interests that lead to it. . . ." But why introduce arguments about the *economic* premises of the abolition of national oppression, which we heard long ago and do not dispute, into a discussion on *one* of the forms of *political* oppression, namely, the forcible retention of one nation within the state boundaries of another nation? This is simply an attempt to evade political questions! The arguments that follow still further strengthen us in this opinion:

"We have no reason to assume that the nation in socialist society will represent an economic-political unit. In all probability it will merely represent a cultural and language unit, since the territorial division of the socialist cultural circle, in so far as it will exist at all, can take place only in accordance with the requirements of production, and the question of this division must naturally be decided, not by separate nations, each having complete independent power (as is demanded by 'the right to self-determination') but *jointly* by all the citizens interested. . . ."

This last argument, about *joint* determination instead of self-determination, pleases the Polish comrades so much that they repeat it *three times* in their theses! But frequent repetition does not change this Octobrist and reactionary argument into a Social-

87

Democratic one, for all reactionaries and the bourgeois grant the nations forcibly retained within the boundaries of a given state the right "jointly to decide" their fate in a common parliament. Wilhelm II also grants the Belgians the right "jointly to decide" in a common German parliament the fate of the German empire.

The very point that is in dispute, the very question that is the exclusive subject of discussion, namely, the right of secession, our opponents attempt to evade. It would be comical were it not so sad!

In our very first thesis it is stated that the liberation of oppressed nationalities presupposes a twofold change in the sphere of politics: (1) Complete equality of all nationalities. There is no dispute about this, and it applies only to what takes place within the state; (2) Freedom of political secession. [17] This concerns the determination of the boundaries of the state. This *alone* is in dispute. And this is the very point our opponents ignore. They refuse to consider the question of state boundaries, or even of the state in general. This is a sort of "Imperialist Economism" similar to the old "Economism" of 1894-1902, which argued in this way: Capital is victorious, *therefore* it is no use raising political questions. Imperialism is victorious, *therefore* it is no use raising political questions! Such a political theory is essentially hostile to Marxism.

In his *Critique of the Gotha Programme* Marx wrote:

"Between capitalist and communist society lies the period of the revolutionary transformation of the one into the other. There corresponds to this also a political transition period in which the state can be nothing but *the revolutionary dictatorship of the proletariat.*" [18]

Up to now this axiom has never been disputed by Socialists, and yet it implies the recognition of the existence of the *state* right up to the time when victorious socialism has grown into complete communism. Engels' dictum about the *withering away* of the state is well known. In our very first thesis we purposely emphasized that democracy is a form of state that will also wither away when the state withers away.

And until our opponents have substituted for Marxism some new "non-state" point of view, we must say that their argument is thoroughly mistaken.

Instead of speaking about the state (and *consequently,* about defining its *boundaries!*), they speak of a "socialist cultural circle," *i.e.,* they deliberately select a vague expression which obliterates all questions concerning the state. What results is ridiculous tautology; of course, if there is no state, there can be no question of its boundaries. That being the case, the *whole* democratic political program is superfluous. Nor will there be a republic when the state "withers away."

The German chauvinist, Lensch, in articles to which we refer in thesis No. 5 (note), [19] quoted an interesting passage from Engels' *The Po and the Rhine*. In this work Engels says, *inter alia,* that the boundaries of "great and virile European nations," which in the course of historical development have absorbed a number of small and devitalized nations, have been determined more and more "by the language and sympathies" of the population. Those boundaries Engels calls "natural" boundaries. This is what occurred in the epoch of progressive capitalism in Europe, approximately between 1848 and 1871. At the present time reactionary imperialist capitalism is more and more often *breaking down* these democratically determined boundaries. All symptoms show that imperialism will leave to its successor, socialism, a heritage of *less* democratic boundaries, a number of annexations in Europe and in other parts of the globe. Well, will victorious socialism in restoring democracy and applying it logically all along the line, reject *democratic means* of determining the boundaries of a state? Will it refuse to take the "sympathies" of the population into consideration? One has only to put these questions to see plainly that our Polish colleagues are slipping from Marxism into "imperialist economism."

The old "economists," distorting Marxism into a caricature, taught the workers that "only" "economics" is important for Marxists. The new "Economists" either assume that the democratic state of victorious socialism will exist without boundaries (like a "complex of sensations" with matter), or that the boundaries will be drawn "only" in accordance with the requirements of production. As a matter of fact, those boundaries will be drawn democratically, *i.e.,* in accordance with the wishes and the "sympathies" of the population. Capitalism violates these sympathies and thus creates fresh obstacles to the establishment of intimacy between nations. Socialism, by organizing production *without* class oppression and by ensuring the well-being of *all* members of the state, gives *full scope* to the "sympathies" of the population, and precisely by virtue of this facilitates and enormously accelerates the establishment of intimacy among and amalgamation of nations.

In order to relieve the reader somewhat of this tiresome and clumsy "Economism," we shall quote the arguments of a Socialist writer who is not involved in our controversy. This writer is Otto Bauer, who has a "kink" of his own, namely, "cultural-national autonomy," but who reasons very correctly on a number of very important questions. For instance, in § 29 of his book, *The National Question and Social-Democracy,* he rightly points out that nationalist ideology may serve as a screen for *imperialist* policy. In § 30, "Socialism and the Principle of Nationalism," he says:

"A socialist community will never be able forcibly to retain whole nations within its boundaries. Picture to yourselves whole masses of people possessing all the advantages of national culture, fully and actively participating in legislation and administration and equipped with arms—would it be possible forcibly to subject such nations to the rule of an alien social organism? Every state power rests on the force of arms. The people's army of today, thanks to cunning machinations, is still a weapon in the hands of a definite person, family or class, just as the armies of knights and mercenaries were in the past. The army of the democratic community in socialist society would be nothing more nor less than the armed nation, for it would consist of highly cultured people, working voluntarily in public workshops and fully participating in all fields of the life of the state. Under such conditions, all possibility of alien national rule disappears."

This is true. It is *impossible,* under capitalism, to abolish national (or any political) oppression. To do this it is *necessary* to abolish classes, *i.e.,* introduce socialism. However, although based on economics, socialism is by no means exclusively economics. To abolish national oppression a foundation is necessary, namely, socialist production; but on this foundation a democratically organized state, a democratic army, etc., must *also* be built. By transforming capitalism into socialism, the proletariat creates the *possibility* for the complete abolition of national oppression; this possibility will become *reality* "only"—"only"—when complete democracy is introduced in all spheres, including the fixing of state boundaries in accordance with the "sympathies" of the population, and including complete freedom of secession. This, in turn, will, *in practice,* lead to the complete elimination of all national friction, of all national suspicion, to the speedy establishment of intimacy between and amalgamation of nations, culminating in the *"withering away"* of the state. This is the theory of Marxism from which our Polish colleagues have mistakenly departed.

IS DEMOCRACY "FEASIBLE" UNDER IMPERIALISM?

All the old polemics of the Polish Social-Democrats against self-determination of nations are based on the argument that it is "infeasible" under capitalism. As far back as 1903, we Iskra-ists ridiculed that argument, in the debates that took place in the Program Committee of the Second Congress of the R.S.D.L.P., and declared that it was a repetition of the caricature of Marxism for which the "Economists" (of sad memory) were responsible. In our theses we dealt with this error in particular detail; but on this point, around which the whole of our theoretical controversy is centered, the Polish comrades have not (or could not?) replied to a *single one* of our arguments.

The economic impossibility of self-determination ought to have been proved by an economic analysis, just as we proved the impracticability of prohibiting machinery, or of introducing labor money, etc. No one has even attempted to make such an analysis. No one will assert that any capitalist country, even as an "exception," has succeeded in introducing "labor money" in the way a certain small country, by way of exception, has succeeded, in the era of most unbridled imperialism, in achieving the unachievable self-determination, even without a war or a revolution (Norway, 1905).

Generally speaking, political democracy is only one of the possible *forms* (although, theoretically, the normal form of "pure" capitalism) of the superstructure that rises *over* capitalism. Facts have proved that both capitalism and imperialism develop under *all* political forms, and subordinate *all of them* to their rule. It is therefore a fundamental theoretical mistake to speak of *one* of the forms and of *one* of the demands of democracy as being "infeasible."

As our Polish colleagues have not replied to these arguments we must consider the discussion on this point closed. In order to bring the point out in greater relief, as it were, we made the definite assertion that it would be "ridiculous" to deny the "feasibility" of restoring Poland at the present time because of strategic and other considerations in the present war. But no reply was forthcoming!

The Polish comrades simply *repeated* an obviously inaccurate assertion (§ II, 1) when they said: "In the matter of annexing foreign territory the forms of political democracy are eliminated; open violence decides. . . . Capital will never allow the people to decide the question of their state boundaries. . . ."

As if "capital" could "allow the people" to select *its* public officials, whose business it is to serve imperialism! Or as if, *in general,* the settlement of any important question of democracy, such as a republic instead of a monarchy, a militia instead of a standing army is conceivable without "open violence"! Subjectively, the Polish comrades want to make Marxism "more profound," but they do it very awkwardly. *Objectively,* their phrases about infeasibility are an expression of opportunism, for it is tacitly assumed: "infeasible" without a series of revolutions, just as *complete* democracy, *all* the demands of democracy in general, are infeasible under imperialism.

Only once, at the very end of § II, 1, in their argument on Alsace, did our Polish colleagues relinquish the position of "Imperialist Economism" and give a definite answer to the question of one of the forms of democracy instead of a general reference to "economics." And on this one occasion they were wrong! It would be "particularist," "undemocratic," they write, if the Alsatians *alone* without asking the French, were to insist on the annexation of Alsace by France, in spite of the fact that part of Alsace gravitated towards the Germans, and that this might give rise to war!!! This is a most amusing tangle: self-determination presupposes (this is self-evident, and we especially emphasized this in our theses) the freedom of *secession* from the oppressing state. In politics it is no more the "custom" to speak about a country *consenting* to annex another than it is the custom in economics to speak about the capitalist "consenting" to receive profits, or of the workers "consenting" to receive wages! It is ridiculous to speak about this.

To be a Marxist political thinker one must, in discussing Alsace, attack the scoundrels of German Socialism for not fighting for freedom of secession for Alsace, attack the scoundrels of French Socialism for reconciling themselves with the French bourgeoisie, which desires forcibly to annex the whole of Alsace, and attack both for serving the imperialism of "their" respective countries fearing a separate state, even a small one; one must show *how* the Socialists, by recognizing self-determination, could solve the problem in a few weeks without running counter to the wishes of the Alsatians. To argue instead about the terrible danger of the French Alsatians "thrusting themselves" on France is a perfect gem.

WHAT ARE ANNEXATIONS?

We put this question very definitely in our theses (§ 7).[20] The Polish comrades have *not* answered the question, they have *evaded* it, declaring very strongly that: (1) they are opposed to annexations, and (2) explaining why they are opposed to them. True, these are very important questions; but they are *not* the questions we are discussing. If we are at all concerned about our principles being theoretically thought out and clearly and precisely formulated, we cannot *evade* the question of what annexations are once we employ this term in our political propaganda and agitation. The evasion of this question in a discussion among colleagues cannot be interpreted otherwise than as a surrender of one's position.

Why did we raise this question? We explained why when we raised it. Because "a protest against annexations is nothing more nor less than recognition of the right to self-determination." The term annexations ordinarily includes: (1) the concept of force (forcible incorporation); (2) the concept of alien oppression (incorporation of an *"alien"* territory, etc.), and sometimes (3) the concept of violating the *status quo*. This we pointed out in our theses and it met with no criticism.

The question arises: Can Social-Democrats be opposed to violence in general? Obviously not. Hence, we are opposed to annexations, not because they are based on violence, but for some other reason. Similarly, Social-Democrats cannot be in favor of the *status quo*. Try as you will, you cannot avoid this conclusion: Annexations *violate self-determination* of nations; they establish state *boundaries against the wishes of the population*.

Being opposed to annexations *means* being in favor of the right to self-determination. Being "opposed to the forcible retention of any nation within the boundaries of a given state" (we deliberately employed *this* slightly modified formulation of the very same idea in § 4 of our theses,[21] and our Polish comrades *quite* definitely replied to it in § 1, 4 of their theses, at the beginning, by saying that they were "opposed to the forcible retention of oppressed nations within the boundaries of the annexing state") is *exactly the same* as being in favor of self-determination of nations.

We do not want to argue about words. If there is a party which states in its program (or in a resolution binding on all, the form is immaterial) that it is opposed to annexations,* opposed to the forcible

---

* In one of his articles in the *Berner Tagwacht*, K. Radek formulated this as "opposed to old and new annexations." See p. 66 of this volume.—*Ed.*

retention of oppressed nations within the boundaries of *its* state, then we declare that in principle we are in complete agreement with that party. It would be absurd to cling to the *word* "self-determination." And if any one were found in our party who desired to change the *wording* of § 9 of our party program in this sense, we would not regard our disagreement with *that* comrade as being one on principle.

All we are concerned about is that our slogans shall be politically clear and theoretically well thought out. In the oral discussions on this question, the importance of which nobody denies, especially now in connection with the war, we met with the following argument (which we have not found in the press); to *protest against* a certain evil does not necessarily imply the recognition of the positive concept which eliminates that evil. This argument is obviously unsound, and evidently for this reason has not been expressed in the press. If a Socialist Party declares itself to be "opposed to the forcible retention of an oppressed nation within the boundaries of an annexing state," the party *thereby undertakes to abandon forcible retention* when it comes into power.

We do not doubt for one moment that if Hindenburg were to achieve a semi-victory over Russia tomorrow, and if the semi-victory found expression (in view of the desire of England and France to weaken tsarism somewhat) in the establishment of a new Polish state, which is quite "feasible" from the standpoint of the economic laws of capitalism and imperialism, and if the socialist revolution were victorious in St. Petersburg, Berlin, and Warsaw the day after tomorrow, the Polish Socialist government, like the Russian and the German governments, would abandon the "forcible retention" of the Ukrainians, say, "within the boundaries of the Polish state." If the members of the editorial board of *Gazeta Robotnicza* are members of this government, they will undoubtedly sacrifice their "theses" and thereby refute the "theory" that "the right to self-determination is inapplicable to socialist society." If we thought otherwise, we would not engage in a comradely discussion with the Social-Democrats of Poland, but would fight them ruthlessly as chauvinists.

Suppose I were to go out in the street of any European city and publicly "protest," and then repeat the "protest" in the newspapers, against being prevented from buying a slave. Undoubtedly, people would be right in regarding me as a slave-owner, an adherent of the principle, or system, if you will, of slavery. The fact that my sympathies in favor of slavery are clothed in the negative form of a protest and not in a positive form ("I am in favor of slavery") will deceive nobody. A political "protest" is *fully* equivalent to a political program; this is so obvious that one almost feels ashamed to have to explain it. At any rate, we are firmly convinced that the Zimmerwald Lefts at least (we do not speak of all the Zimmerwaldists, for among them are Martov and other Kautskyists), will not "protest" when we say that there will be no place in the Third International for those who draw a distinction between a political protest and a political program, who oppose one to the other, etc.

Not wishing to argue about words, we express the firm hope that the Polish Social-Democrats will soon make an effort to formulate officially their proposal that § 9 be deleted from our (and also *their*) party program and from the program of the International (resolution of the London Congress of 1896), as well as *their own* definition of the respective political concepts of "old and new annexations" and of "forcible retention of an oppressed nation within the boundaries of the annexing state." We will pass to the next question.

FOR OR AGAINST ANNEXATIONS?

In § 3 of the first section of their theses, the Polish comrades very definitely declare that they are opposed to all annexations. Unfortunately, § 4 of the same section contains statements which we must regard as annexationist. This paragraph begins with the following— shall we say strange, to put it mildly?—sentence:

"The starting point of Social-Democracy's struggle against annexations, against the forcible retention of oppressed nations within the boundaries of an annexing state, is *repudiation of defense of the fatherland in every form*" (authors' italics), "which in the era of imperialism is defense of the right of the bourgeoisie of one's own country to oppress and rob other nations. . . ."

What is this? Why?

"The starting point of the struggle against annexations is repudiation of defense of the fatherland *in every form*. . . ." But the term "defense of the fatherland" may be applied, and hitherto has been *commonly* applied, to every national war and every national rebellion! We are opposed to annexations, *but* . . . we understand this to mean that we are opposed to war waged by annexed countries *for* their liberation from those who have annexed them; we are opposed to the annexed countries rising in rebellion in order to liberate themselves from those who have annexed them! Is this not an annexationist assertion?

The argument the authors of this strange assertion advanced in support of it is that "in the era of imperialism" defense of the fatherland is defense of the right of the bourgeoisie of one's country to oppress foreign nations. But this is true *only* in respect of an imperialist war, *i.e.*, a war *between* imperialist powers or groups of powers, when *each* belligerent is not only oppressing "foreign nations" but is waging the war *in order* to impose its yoke on *more* foreign nations!

Evidently the authors present the question of "defense of the fatherland" quite differently from the way our party presents it. We repudiate "defense of the fatherland" in an *imperialist* war. This is stated as clearly as it can be in the manifesto of the Central Committee of our party and in the Berne resolutions,[22] both of which were reproduced in the pamphlet, *Socialism and War*, published in German and French. *Twice* we emphasized this in our theses (notes to §4 and §6).[23] The authors of the Polish theses evidently reject defense of the fatherland in *general, i.e.*, also in a *national war*, assuming probably, that national wars are *impossible* "in the era of imperialism." We say "probably" because the Polish comrades have *not* expressed such views in their theses.

This view, however, is clearly expressed in the theses of the German International group and in Junius' pamphlet, to which we devote a special article.[24] In addition to what we said in that article we wish to note that a national rebellion of an annexed territory, or country, against the country which has annexed it may be described as a rebellion and not a war (we have heard this view expressed and that is why we refer to it, although we regard this controversy over terminology as frivolous). At all events, hardly any one will dare deny that annexed Belgium, Serbia, Galicia, Armenia will describe, *and rightly describe,* their "rebellion" against the countries which have annexed them as "defense of the fatherland." It follows that our Polish comrades are *opposed* to such a rebellion on the ground that there is *also* a bourgeoisie in the annexed countries, and that this bourgeoisie *also* oppresses other nations, or rather, it *may* oppress them, since the only point under discussion is "*right* to oppress." It appears, then, that the criterion of a given war, or a given rebellion, is not its *real* social content (the struggle of an oppressed nation against the oppressor for liberation), but the possibility of the now oppressed bourgeoisie exercising its "*right* to oppress." If, for example, Belgium were annexed by Germany in 1917 and rose in rebellion for its liberty in 1918, the Polish comrades

96

would oppose the rebellion on the ground that the Belgian bourgeoisie had "the right to oppress foreign nations"!

There is not a trace of Marxian, or of revolutionary thinking, in general, in this line of argument. If we do not want to betray socialism, we *must* support *every* rebellion against our main enemy, the bourgeoisie of the big states, provided it is not the rebellion of a reactionary class. By refusing to support rebellions of annexed territories we objectively become annexationists. Precisely "in the era of imperialism," which is the era of the incipient social revolution, the proletariat makes special efforts to support the rebellion of annexed territories today, in order that tomorrow, or simultaneously with the rebellion, it may attack the bourgeoisie of the "Great" Power which is weakened by that rebellion.

The Polish comrades, however, go still further in their annexationism. They are not only opposed to rebellions of annexed territories, they are also opposed to the restoration of their independence in *any* way, even peacefully! Listen to this:

"Social-Democracy, rejecting all responsibility for the consequences of the imperialist policy of oppression, and combating it in the sharpest possible manner, *under no circumstances supports the establishment of new frontier posts in Europe, the restoration of the barriers swept away by imperialism.*" (Authors' italics.)

At the present time "imperialism has swept away the frontier posts" between Germany and Belgium, between Russia and Galicia. But, you see, international Social-Democracy must, in general, oppose the restoration of these frontier posts in any way whatever. When, in 1905, "in the era of imperialism," the autonomous Diet of Norway, which was advocated by the Swedish reactionaries, was prevented by the resistance of the Swedish workers and also by the international imperialist situation, Social-Democracy should have opposed the secession of Norway on the ground that it undoubtedly meant the "establishment of new frontier posts in Europe"!!

This is downright annexationism. There is no need to refute it, it refutes itself. No Socialist Party would dare to take up the position that "we are opposed to annexations in general, but as far as Europe is concerned, we sanction annexations, or reconcile ourselves to them when they are carried out. . . ."

It is necessary to examine only the theoretical source of the error which has brought our Polish comrades to such a self-evident . . . "impossibility." Later on we will show that it is wrong to single out "Europe." The following two passages of the theses explain other sources of the error:

". . . Where the wheel of imperialism has passed over an already established capitalist state and has crushed it, there the political and economic concentration of the capitalist world takes place in the brutal form of imperialist oppression, paving the way for socialism. . . ."

This justification of annexation is Struveism, not Marxism. Russian Social-Democrats who remember the 'nineties in Russia are quite familiar with this method of distorting Marxism commonly adopted by Messrs. Struve, Cunow, Legien and Co. It is precisely with reference to the German Struveists, the so-called "social-imperialists," that we read the following in another part of our Polish comrades' theses (II, 3):

(The slogan of self-determination) "enables the social-imperialists, by proving the illusory character of this slogan, to represent our struggle against national oppression as historically unsound sentimentality, and thus to undermine the confidence of the proletariat in the scientific soundness of the Social-Democratic program."

This implies that the authors regard the position taken up by the German Struveists as "scientific"! We congratulate them!

But this astonishing argument, which threatened to prove that the Lensches, Cunows, and Parvuses are *right* and that we are wrong, is shattered by the following "trifle," namely, that these Lensches are, in their way, consistent, and in No. 8-9 of the German chauvinist *Glocke*—we deliberately quoted these issues in our theses— Lensch *simultaneously* proves the "scientific unsoundness" of the slogan of self-determination (the Polish Social-Democrats have evidently accepted *this* argument of Lensche's as being irrefutable, as is apparent from the argument we have quoted from their theses . . .) *and* the "scientific unsoundness" of the slogan: against annexations!!

For Lensch understands perfectly the simple truth which we pointed out to our Polish colleagues who refused to reply to our argument, namely, that there is no difference, "either economic or political," nor any logical difference, between "recognizing" self-determination and "protesting" against annexations. If the Polish comrades regard Lensch's arguments against self-determination as irrefutable, then they cannot but admit the *fact* that the Lensches also direct *all* these arguments against the struggle against annexations.

The theoretical error which lies at the root of all the arguments advanced by our Polish colleagues has brought them to the position of *inconsistent annexationists*.

WHY IS SOCIAL-DEMOCRACY OPPOSED
TO ANNEXATIONS?

From our point of view, the answer is clear. We are opposed to annexations because they violate the right of self-determination of nations or, in other words, are one of the forms of national oppression.

From the point of view of the Polish Social-Democrats, it is necessary to give some *special* explanation as to why we are opposed to annexations, and these explanations (1, 3 in the theses) inevitably involve the authors in a new series of contradictions.

They advance two arguments to "justify" our opposition to annexations (notwithstanding the "scientifically sound" arguments of the Lensches). The first is:

"... To the assertion that annexations in Europe are necessary for the military security of the victorious imperialist state, Social-Democracy opposes the fact that annexations only intensify antagonisms and thereby increase the danger of war...."

This answer to the Lensches is inadequate, for their main argument is not military necessity, but the *economically* progressive character of annexations, which mean concentration under imperialism. Where is the logic of the Polish Social-Democrats when at one and the same time they admit that *such* concentration is progressive, oppose the restoration in Europe of the frontier posts which have been swept away by imperialism, and *object* to annexations?

To proceed. Annexations increase the danger of *what kind* of wars? Not imperialist wars, because they are engendered by other causes. The main antagonisms in the present imperialist war are indisputably the antagonisms between England and Germany, Russia and Germany. The question of annexations was never involved here. The question here is the increase in the danger of *national* wars and national rebellions. But how is it possible, on the one hand, to declare that national wars are *impossible* "in the era of imperialism" and, on the other hand, to point to the "danger" of national wars? This is not logical.

The second argument:

(Annexations) "create a gulf between the proletariat of the ruling nation and that of the oppressed nation. ... The proletariat of the oppressed nation would unite with its bourgeoisie and would regard the proletariat of the ruling nation as its enemy. Instead of the international class war of the proletariat against the international bourgeoisie there would be a split in the ranks of the proletariat, it would become ideologically corrupted. . . ."

We fully accept these arguments. But is it logical, in discussing a given question, simultaneously to advance arguments which mutually exclude each other? In § 3, section 1 of the theses we read the above-quoted argument about annexations causing a *split* in the ranks of the proletariat, and in the very next paragraph, § 4, we are told that in Europe we must oppose the annulment of annexations already effected and "educate the masses of the workers of both the oppressed and the oppressing nations for a united struggle." If the annulment of annexations is reactionary "sentimentality," it *cannot* be argued that annexations create a "gulf" in the midst of the "proletariat" and cause a "split" in its ranks. On the contrary, from this point of view annexations should be regarded as a condition for bringing the proletariat of various nations *closer together*.

We say: In order that we may be able to bring about the socialist revolution and overthrow the bourgeoisie, the workers must unite more closely, and this close unity is facilitated by the struggle for self-determination, *i.e.*, against annexations. We are consistent. Our Polish comrades, however, by accepting the "non-annulment" of annexations in Europe and by arguing that national wars are "impossible," contradict themselves when, in arguing "against" annexations, they use arguments that *pertain to* national wars! Arguments of the kind that annexations *hinder* the establishment of intimacy between and the amalgamation of the workers of different nations!

In other words, in order to oppose annexations, the Polish Social-Democrats are compelled to take their arguments from that theoretical armory which *they themselves* reject on principle.

This is even more apparent in the question of the colonies.

CAN THE COLONIES BE CONTRASTED WITH "EUROPE" ON THIS QUESTION?

In our theses we said that the demand for the immediate liberation of the colonies is just as "infeasible" (*i.e.*, infeasible without a series of revolutions and transient without socialism) under capitalism as self-determination of nations, or the election of public officials by the people, or a democratic republic, etc.—and on the other hand, that the demand for the liberation of the colonies is nothing more nor less than the "recognition of the self-determination of nations."

100

The Polish comrades have not replied to either of these arguments. They tried to draw a distinction between "Europe" and the colonies. Only in regard to Europe are they inconsistent annexationists and object to the annulment of annexations once they have been effected. For the colonies, however, they put forward the categorical demand: "Get out of the colonies!"

Russian Socialists must put forward the demand: "Get out of Turkestan, Khiva, Bokhara, etc.," but they would sink into "utopianism," into "unscientific sentimentality," etc., if they were to demand the same freedom of secession for Poland, Finland, Ukraine, etc. English Socialists must put forward the demand: "Get out of Africa, India, Australia," but not out of Ireland. What theoretical arguments can explain such a glaringly wrong distinction? This question cannot be evaded.

The main "base" of the opponents of self-determination is "infeasibility." The same idea, slightly different in shade, is expressed by the reference to "economic and political concentration."

It is clear that concentration takes place *also* by means of the annexation of colonies. Formerly, the economic difference between colonies and the European nations—at least the majority of them— was that the colonies had been drawn into the sphere of exchange of *commodities,* but not yet into the sphere of capitalist *production.* Imperialism has changed this. Imperialism, among other things, means the export of *capital.* Capitalist production is more and more rapidly being transplanted to the colonies. It is impossible to liberate them from their dependence upon European finance capital. From a military point of view, as well as from the point of view of expansion, the secession of the colonies can, as a general rule, be achieved only with the advent of socialism; whereas under capitalism it is possible, either as an exception, or as the result of a series of revolutions and rebellions in the colonies and in the mother country.

In Europe, most of the dependent nations (though not all of them—for example, the Albanians and many native peoples of Russia) are capitalistically more developed than the colonies. But it is this very fact that gives rise to greater resistance to national oppression and annexations! It is precisely for this reason that the development of capitalism is more *secure* in Europe, under all political conditions, including secession, than it is in the colonies. ... "There," the Polish comrades say of the colonies (1, 4), "capitalism is still confronted with the task of independently developing the productive forces. . . ." In Europe this is still more marked: capitalism in Poland, in Finland, in the Ukraine, and in Alsace is undoubtedly developing the productive forces more strongly, more rapidly and more independently than in India, Turkestan, Egypt, and other colonies of the purest type. Neither independent nor any other kind of development is possible without capital in a society based on commodity production. The dependent nations of Europe have *their own* capital, and they can easily acquire more capital on the most diverse terms. The colonies, however, have no capital of *their own,* or almost none, and under the rule of finance capital a colony cannot obtain capital except at the price of political subjugation. In view of all this, what is the sense of demanding the immediate and unconditional liberation of the colonies? Is it not obvious that it is much more "utopian," in that vulgar, caricature-of-"Marxism" sense of the word in which it is employed by the Struves, Lensches, Cunows and, following them, also, unfortunately, by our Polish comrades? There the word "utopian" is taken to mean departure from the ordinary, including everything revolutionary. The fact is that revolutionary movements of *all* kinds—including national movements—are, under the conditions prevailing in Europe, more likely, more possible, more stubborn, more conscious and more difficult to subdue than in the colonies.

Socialism, say the Polish comrades (1, 3) "will be able to give to the backward peoples in the colonies *unselfish cultural aid without ruling over* them." This is perfectly true. But what grounds are there for believing that a great nation, a great state, having passed over to socialism, will not be able to attract to itself a small oppressed nation in Europe by means of "unselfish cultural aid"? It is precisely the freedom of secession, which the Polish Social-Democrats *"grant"* the colonies, that will draw the small, but culturally and politically *exacting,* oppressed nations of Europe into an alliance with the great socialist states, for a big state under socialism would mean so many hours of work *less* every day, and so much *more earnings* every day. Liberated from the yoke of the bourgeoisie, the masses of the toilers will *strive* with all their might to ally themselves with the great advanced socialist nations for the sake of this "cultural aid," if only the quondam oppressors do not offend the highly developed democratic sense of self-respect of the long oppressed nations, if only they grant them equality in everything, including state construction, experience in constructing "their own" state. Under capitalism, this "experience" means wars, isolation, insularity, narrow selfishness on the part of the privileged small nations (Holland, Switzerland). Under socialism, the masses of the toilers themselves, for the purely economic reasons mentioned above, will refuse to agree to insularity, whereas the variety of political forms, the freedom to secede from the state, experience in state construction—all this will, until the state itself withers away, be the basis for a rich cultured life, the guarantee of an acceleration of the voluntary establishment of intimacy between and amalgamation of nations.

By singling out the colonies and contrasting them with Europe, the Polish comrades become involved in contradictions, which immediately shatter the whole of their mistaken line of argument.

MARXISM OR PROUDHONISM?

Quite as an exception, our Polish comrades parry our reference to Marx's attitude towards the separation of Ireland not by inference, but directly. What is their objection? In their opinion, references to the position Marx held from 1848 to 1871 are "not of the slightest value." The argument advanced in support of this unusually irate and positive assertion is that Marx "at one and the same time" expressed opposition to the strivings for independence of the "Czechs, South Slavs, etc."*

The argument is so very irate because it is so very unsound. According to the Polish Marxists, Marx was simply a muddlehead who "at one and the same time" said contradictory things! This is altogether untrue, and it is altogether un-Marxist. The "concrete" analysis upon which our Polish comrades insist, *but do not themselves apply,* obliges us to investigate whether the different attitudes Marx adopted towards different concrete "national" movements did not spring from *one and the same* socialist *philosophy.*

As is generally known, Marx was in favor of Polish independence in the interests of *European* democracy in its struggle against the power and influence—we may say, against the omnipotence and predominating reactionary influence—of tsarism. That this attitude was correct was most clearly and practically demonstrated in 1849, when the Russian serf army crushed the national liberation and revolutionary-democratic rebellion in Hungary. From that time until Marx's death, and even later, until 1890, when there was a danger that tsarism, allied with France, would wage a reactionary war against a *non-imperialist* but nationally independent Germany, Engels stood first and foremost for a struggle against tsarism. It was for this reason, and exclusively for this reason, that Marx and

* The reference is to "Democratic Pan-Slavism," an article in the *Neue Rheinische Zeitung,* of February 14-15, 1849.—*Ed.*

Engels were opposed to the national movement of the Czechs and South Slavs. A simple comparison with what Marx and Engels wrote in 1848 and 1849 will prove to any one who is interested in Marxism, not merely in order to brush Marxism aside, that Marx and Engels at that time drew a clear and definite *distinction* between "whole reactionary peoples" serving as "Russian outposts" in Europe, and "revolutionary peoples," namely, the Germans, Poles, and Magyars. This is a fact. And this fact was indicated *at the time with incontrovertible* truth: in 1848 revolutionary peoples fought for liberty, the principal enemy of which was tsarism, whereas the Czechs, etc., were really reactionary nations, outposts of tsarism.

What does this concrete example, which must be analyzed *concretely* if one wishes to be true to Marxism, imply? Only this: (1) that the interests of the liberation of a number of big and very big nations in Europe stand higher than the interests of the movement for liberation of small nations; (2) that a democratic demand must not be considered in isolation, but on a European—today we should say a world—scale.

Nothing more. There is not a hint in this of repudiation of the elementary socialist principle which the Poles are forgetting, but to which Marx was *always* faithful, namely, that no nation can be free if it oppresses other nations. If the concrete situation which confronted Marx in the epoch when tsarist influence was predominant in international politics were to repeat itself, for instance, in such a form that a number of nations were to start a socialist revolution (as a bourgeois-democratic revolution was started in Europe in 1848), while *other* nations serve as the chief bulwarks of bourgeois reaction—then we would have to be in favor of a revolutionary war against the latter, in favor of "crushing" them, in favor of destroying all their outposts, no matter what small national movements arose there. Consequently, we must not discard examples of Marx's tactics—this would mean professing Marxism in words while discarding it in practice—we must analyze them concretely and draw invaluable lessons from them for the future. The various demands of democracy, including self-determination, are not absolute, but a *small* part of the general democratic (now: general Socialist) *world* movement. Possibly, in individual concrete cases, the part may contradict the whole; if so, it must be rejected. It is possible that the republican movement in one country may be merely an instrument of the clerical or financial-monarchical intrigues of other countries; if so, we must *not* support this particular, concrete movement. But it would be ridiculous on these grounds to delete the demand for a republic from the program of international Social-Democracy.

In what way has the concrete situation changed from 1848-71 to 1898-1916 (I take the most important landmarks of imperialism as a period; from the Spanish-American imperialist war to the European imperialist war)? Tsarism had obviously and incontrovertibly ceased to be the chief mainstay of reaction, first, because it is supported by international finance capital, particularly French; second, because of 1905. At that time the system of big national states—the democracies of Europe—brought democracy and socialism to the world in spite of tsarism. Marx and Engels did not live to see the period of imperialism. At the present time a system of a handful of imperialist "Great" Powers (five or six in number) has come into being, each of which oppresses other nations; and this oppression is one of the sources that is artificially retarding the collapse of capitalism, that is artificially fostering opportunism and social-chauvinism in the imperialist nations which dominate the world. At that time West European democracy, which was liberating the big nations, was opposed to tsarism, which was using certain small national movements for reactionary ends. At the present time an *alliance* between tsarist imperialism and advanced capitalist, European imperialism, based on their general oppression of a number of nations, confronts the Socialist proletariat, which is split into chauvinists, "social-imperialists," and revolutionaries.

Such are the concrete changes that have taken place in the situation, and it is just these that the Polish Social-Democrats ignore, in spite of their promise to be concrete! Hence the concrete change in the *application* of the same Socialist principles: *at that time* first of all "against tsarism" (and against certain small national movements that were being utilized *by it* for anti-democratic ends), and for the big national, revolutionary peoples of the West; *at the present time* against the united, straightened-out front of the imperialist powers, of the imperialist bourgeoisie, of the social-imperialists, and *for* utilizing *all* national movements against imperialism for the purposes of the socialist revolution. The *purer* the proletarian struggle against the general imperialist front now becomes, the more urgent, obviously, becomes the internationalist principle: "No nation can be free if it oppresses other nations."

In the name of a doctrinaire conception of the social revolution, the Proudhonists ignored the international role of Poland and brushed the national movements aside. Equally doctrinaire is the attitude of the Polish Social-Democrats, since they *break* the international front

105

of the struggle against the social-imperialists (objectively) helping the latter by their vacillations on the question of annexations. For it is precisely the international front of the proletarian struggle that has changed in relation to the concrete position of the small nations: at that time (1848-71) the small nations were important as the potential allies either of "Western democracy" and the revolutionary nations, or of tsarism. At the present time (1898-1914) the small nations have lost this importance; their importance now is that they are one of the sources fostering the parasitism and, consequently, the social-imperialism of the "ruling nations." The important thing is not whether one-fiftieth or one-hundredth of the small nations will be liberated before the socialist revolution, but the fact that in the epoch of imperialism, owing to objective causes, the proletariat has been split into two international camps, one of which has been corrupted by the crumbs that fall from the table of the bourgeoisie of the ruling nations—obtained, among other things, from the two-fold or threefold exploitation of small nations—while the other cannot liberate itself without liberating the small nations, without educating the masses in an anti-chauvinist, *i.e.*, anti-annexationist, *i.e.*, "self-determinationist" spirit.

This, the most important aspect of the question, is ignored by the Polish comrades, who do *not* view things from the central position in the epoch of imperialism, from the standpoint that the international proletariat is divided into two camps.

Here are other concrete examples of their Proudhonism: (1) their attitude to the Irish rebellion of 1916, of which we shall speak later; (2) the declaration in the theses (II, 3, at the end of § 3) that the slogan of socialist revolution "must not be obscured by anything." To think that the slogan of socialist revolution can be "obscured" by *combining* it with a consistently revolutionary position on all questions, including the national question, is certainly profoundly anti-Marxist.

The Polish Social-Democrats consider that our program is a "national-reformist" program. Compare the two practical proposals: (1) for autonomy (Polish theses, III, 4), and (2) for freedom of secession. It is here, and here alone, that our programs differ! And is it not evident that the first proposal is reformist and not the second? A reformist change is one which leaves the foundations of the power of the ruling class intact and which is merely a concession by the ruling class that leaves its power unimpaired. A revolutionary change undermines the foundations of power. The reformist proposals in the national program do *not* abolish *all* the privileges of

106

the ruling nation; they do *not* establish complete equality; they do *not* abolish national oppression *in all its forms*. An "autonomous" nation does not enjoy equal rights with the "ruling" nation; the Polish comrades could not have failed to notice this had they not obstinately avoided (like our old "Economists") an analysis of *political* concepts and categories. Until 1905 autonomous Norway, as a part of Sweden, enjoyed the widest autonomy, but it did not enjoy equality with Sweden. Only by its free secession was its equality manifested *in practice* and proved (and let us add in parentheses that it was precisely this free secession that created the basis for a more intimate and democratic friendship founded on equality of rights). As long as Norway was merely autonomous the Swedish aristocracy had *one* additional privilege; and this privilege was not "mitigated" by secession (the essence of reformism lies in *mitigating* an evil and not in destroying it), but *entirely removed* (the principal criterion of the revolutionary character of a program).

Be it noted, in passing, that autonomy as a reform differs in principle from freedom of secession as a revolutionary measure. This goes without saying. But as every one knows, in practice a reform is often merely a step towards revolution. It is precisely autonomy which enables a nation forcibly retained within the boundaries of a given state to constitute itself completely as a nation, to gather, to ascertain and organize its forces, and to select the most opportune moment to *declare* . . . in the "Norwegian" spirit: "We, the autonomous Parliament of such and such a nation, or of such and such a territory, declare that the Emperor of all the Russias has ceased to be King of Poland," etc. To this it is usually "objected" that such questions are decided by wars and not by declarations. True: in the vast majority of cases they are decided by wars (just as the question of the forms of government of big states in the vast majority of cases is decided only by wars and revolutions). However, it would do no harm to reflect and ask: Is *such* an "objection" to the political program of a revolutionary party logical? Are we opposed to wars and revolutions *on behalf of* what is just and beneficial for the proletariat, *on behalf of* democracy and socialism?

"But we cannot be in favor of a war between great nations, in favor of the slaughter of twenty million people for the sake of the problematical liberation of a small nation with a population of perhaps ten or twenty millions!" No, of course we cannot! But not because we throw out of our program complete national equality, but because the interests of the democracy of *one* country must be subordinated to the interests of the democracy of *several* and of

107

all countries. Let us assume that between two great monarchies there is a little monarchy whose kinglet is "bound" by blood and other ties to the monarchs of both neighboring countries. Let us further assume that the declaration of a republic in the little country and the expulsion of *its* monarch would in practice lead to a war between the two neighboring great nations for the restoration of some monarch or other in the little country. There is no doubt that in this case all international Social-Democracy, as well as the really internationalist section of Social-Democracy in the little country, *would be opposed to substituting a republic for the monarchy.* The substitution of a republic for a monarchy is not an absolute, but one of the democratic demands, a demand subordinated to the interests of democracy (and still more, of course, to the interests of the Socialist proletariat) as a whole. In all probability a case like this would not give rise to the slightest disagreement between Social-Democrats in any country. But if any Social-Democrat were to propose on *these* grounds that the demand for a republic be deleted altogether from the program of international Social-Democracy, he would certainly be looked upon as insane. He would be told that the elementary logical difference between the *particular* and the *general* must not be forgotten.

This example brings us, from a somewhat different angle, to the question of the *internationalist* education of the working class. Can such education—about the necessity and urgent importance of which differences of opinion among the Zimmerwald Lefts are inconceivable—be *concretely identical* in great oppressing nations and in small oppressed nations, in annexing nations and in annexed nations?

Obviously not. The way to the one goal—to complete equality, to the closest intimacy and the subsequent *amalgamation of all* nations —obviously proceeds here by different concrete routes; in the same way, let us say, as the route to a point in the middle of a given page lies towards the left from one edge and towards the right from the opposite edge. If a Social-Democrat belonging to a great, oppressing, annexing nation, when advocating the amalgamation of nations in general, were to forget even for one moment that "his" Nicholas II, "his" Wilhelm, George, Poincaré, etc. *also stands for amalgamation* with small nations (by means of annexations)—Nicholas II being for "amalgamation" with Galicia, Wilhelm II for "amalgamation" with Belgium, etc.—such a Social-Democrat would be a ridiculous doctrinaire in theory and an abettor of imperialism in practice.

The weight of emphasis in the internationalist education of the workers of the oppressing countries must necessarily consist in advocating and getting them to demand freedom of secession for oppressed countries. Without this there can be *no* internationalism. It is our right and duty to treat every Social-Democrat of an oppressing nation who *fails* to conduct such propaganda as an imperialist and a scoundrel. This is an absolute demand, even if the *chance* of secession was possible and "feasible" only one in a thousand before the introduction of socialism.

It is our duty to educate the workers to be "indifferent" to national distinctions. Nobody will dispute that. But not to be indifferent in the spirit of the *annexationists*. A member of an oppressing nation must be "indifferent" to whether small nations belong to *his* state or to a *neighboring* state or to themselves, according to where their sympathies lie: if he is not "indifferent" in this way he is *not* a Social-Democrat. To be an internationalist Social-Democrat one must *not* think only of one's own nation, but must place the interests of all nations, their general liberty and equality, *above one's own nation*. In "theory" every one agrees with this, but in practice an annexationist indifference is displayed. Herein lies the root of the evil.

On the contrary, a Social-Democrat belonging to a small nation must place the weight of his agitation on the *second* word in our general formula: "voluntary *amalgamation*" of nations. He may, without violating his duties as an internationalist, be in favor *either* of the political independence of his nation *or* of its inclusion in neighboring state X, Y, Z, etc. But in all cases he must fight *against* small-nation narrow-mindedness, insularity and aloofness, he must fight for the recognition of the whole and the general, and for the subordination of the interests of the particular to the interests of the general.

People who have not gone thoroughly into the question think that there is a "contradiction" in Social-Democrats of oppressing nations insisting on "freedom of *secession*" while Social-Democrats of oppressed nations insist on "freedom of *amalgamation*." However, a little reflection will show that there is not, nor can there be, any *other* road leading from the *given* situation to internationalism and the amalgamation of nations, that there is not, nor can there be, any other road leading to this goal.

This brings us to the *particular* position of Dutch and Polish Social-Democracy.

THE PARTICULAR AND THE GENERAL IN THE
POSITION OF THE DUTCH AND POLISH
INTERNATIONALIST SOCIAL-DEMOCRATS

There is not the slightest doubt that the Dutch and Polish Marxists who are opposed to self-determination belong to the best revolutionary and internationalist elements in international Social-Democracy. How is it, then, that their theoretical reasoning is, as we have seen, just a mass of errors? Not a single correct general argument; nothing but "imperialist economism"!

It is not due to any particularly bad subjective qualities of the Dutch and Polish comrades; it is due to the *special* objective conditions prevailing in their countries. Both countries (1) are small and helpless in the modern "system" of Great Powers; (2) are geographically located between very powerful, predatory imperialist powers between whom rivalry is most acute (England and Germany, Germany and Russia); (3) retain very vivid and strong recollections and traditions of the times when *they themselves* were "Great Powers": Holland was a great colonial power much stronger than England, Poland was a more cultured and stronger nation than Russia or Prussia; (4) up to the present time have retained the privilege of oppressing other peoples; the Dutch bourgeoisie possesses the fabulously rich Dutch East Indies, the Polish landlord oppresses the Ukrainian and Byelorussian peasants, the Polish bourgeoisie oppresses the Jews, etc.

This peculiarity, this combination of the four special conditions, enumerated above, is not to be found in Ireland, Portugal (which at one time was annexed to Spain), Alsace, Norway, Finland, the Ukraine, the Lettish Province, the Byelorussian Province, and many others. And it is in precisely this peculiarity that *the whole essence* of the matter lies. When the Dutch and Polish Social-Democrats advance *general* arguments against self-determination, *i.e.,* arguments about imperialism in general, socialism in general, democracy in general, national oppression in general, we get a long string of errors, each racing after the other, as it were. But as soon as the obviously erroneous *wrappings* of general arguments are removed and the *core* of the question is examined from the standpoint of the peculiarity of the *particular* conditions in Holland and Poland, their peculiar position becomes *intelligible* and perfectly legitimate. Without running the risk of appearing paradoxical, one may say that in their vehement opposition to self-determination the Dutch and

Polish Marxists do not quite say what they mean or, in other words, they do not quite mean what they say.*

We have already quoted one example in our theses.[25] Gorter is opposed to self-determination for *his own country*, but is *in favor* of self-determination for the Dutch East Indies, which is oppressed by "his" nation! Is it surprising that we regard him as a more sincere internationalist and more akin to us in ideas than those who recognise self-determination in words alone, who recognise it hypocritically, as Kautsky does among the Germans, and Trotsky and Martov among us? From the general and fundamental principles of Marxism inevitably follows the duty of fighting for freedom of secession for nations which are oppressed by "my own" nation; but it does not follow that we must fight first of all for the independence of Holland, which suffers most of all from a narrow, hidebound, selfish, and benumbing insularity which says: let the whole world burn, it's not our affair; "we" are satisfied with our old booty and with the rich "little remnant" of it, the Indies; "we" are not concerned with anything else.

Another example: Karl Radek—a Polish Social-Democrat who deserves particular recognition for the determined struggle he has carried on for internationalism in the German Social-Democratic movement since the outbreak of the war—in an article entitled "The Right of Nations to Self-Determination" (published in *Lichtstrahlen* —a Left radical monthly edited by J. Borchardt, suppressed by the Prussian censorship—Dec. 5, 1915, third year, No. 3) vehemently opposes self-determination, quoting by the way, *only* Dutch and Polish authorities to support his arguments, and *inter alia* advances the argument that self-determination fosters the idea that "it is the duty of Social-Democracy to support every struggle for independence."

From the standpoint of *general* theory, this argument is positively outrageous, for it is obviously illogical; first, because there is not, nor can there be, a single partial democratic demand that does not give rise to abuses if the particular is not subordinated to the general; we are not obliged to support "every" struggle for independence or "every" republican or anti-clerical movement. Second, because there is not, nor can there be, a *single* formulation of the struggle against national oppression that does not suffer from *just this* "defect." Radek himself, in the *Berner Tagwacht* (1915, No. 253) used the

* We recall the fact that in their Zimmerwald declaration *all* the Polish Social-Democrats *recognized* self-determination *in general*, only in a slightly different formulation.

111

formula: "Against old and new annexations." Any Polish nationalist will quite legitimately "deduce" from this formula the following: "Poland was annexed, I am opposed to annexations, *therefore* I am for the independence of Poland." Again, Rosa Luxemburg, we remember, in an article written in 1908, expressed the opinion that the formula "against national oppression" was sufficient. But any Polish nationalist will say—*and quite rightly*—that annexation is *one* of the forms of national oppression, *therefore,* etc.

Instead of these general arguments, however, take the *particular* position of Poland: her independence is *at present* "unachievable" without wars or revolutions. To be in favor of a general European war merely for the sake of restoring Polish independence means being a nationalist of the worst brand; means putting the interests of a small number of Poles above the interests of hundreds of millions of people who would suffer from the war. Such indeed, are, for instance the "Fraki" (Right wing of the Polish Socialist Party) who are Socialists only in words, compared with whom the Polish Socialist-Democrats are a thousand times right. To advance the slogan of Polish independence *at the present time,* bearing in mind the relationships *at present* existing between the *neighboring* imperialist nations, really means chasing after a utopia, sinking into narrow-minded nationalism, forgetting the prerequisites for a general European, or at least a Russian and German, revolution. Similarly, advancing as a separate slogan the demand for freedom of association in the Russia of 1908-14, meant chasing after a utopia, thereby, objectively, aiding the Stolypin labor party (now the party of Potresov and Gvozdev, which is just the same thing). It would have been madness, however, to have deleted the demand for freedom of association from the program of Social-Democracy!

The third, and perhaps, the most important example: in the Polish theses (III, end of 2), in an argument against the idea of an independent Polish buffer state, we read that this is:

". . . an idle utopia entertained by small, impotent groups. If realized, this idea would mean the creation of a small, fragmentary Polish state, which would be a military colony of one or other group of Great Powers, a plaything of their military and economic interests, a field of exploitation by foreign capital, a battlefield in future wars."

All this is very *true in opposition* to the slogan of Polish independence *at the present time,* for even a revolution in Poland alone would not alter anything, while the attention of the Polish masses would be diverted from the *main* thing: from the connection be-

112

tween their struggle and the struggle of the Russian and German proletariat. It is not a paradox, but a fact, that the Polish proletariat, as such, can now aid the cause of socialism and freedom, *including that of Poland,* only by fighting *in conjunction* with the proletariat of the neighboring countries against the *narrow Polish* nationalists. It cannot be denied that in the struggle against the latter, the Polish Social-Democrats have rendered historically important service.

But the very arguments which are correct from the standpoint of the *particular* position of Poland in the *present* epoch are obviously incorrect in the *general* form in which they are presented. Poland will always be a battlefield in the wars between Germany and Russia as long as wars are waged; this is not an argument against greater political freedom (and, consequently, against political independence) in periods between wars. The same holds true concerning the argument about exploitation by alien capital, about being a plaything in the hands of alien interests. The Polish Social-Democrats cannot, at present, advance the slogan of Polish independence, because, as proletarian internationalists, the Poles can do *nothing* to achieve it without, like the "Fraki," sinking into mean servility to *one* of the imperialist monarchies. To the Russian and German workers, however, it is *not* a matter of indifference whether they participate in the annexation of Poland (which would mean educating the German and Russian workers and peasants in the spirit of most despicable servility, of reconciliation with the role of hangman of other peoples), or whether Poland is independent.

Undoubtedly, the situation is very complicated, but there is a way out which enables *all* the participants to remain internationalists: the Russian and the German Social-Democrats must demand unconditional "*freedom* of secession" for Poland; the Polish Social-Democrats must fight for the unity of the proletarian struggle in small and big countries, without advancing, in the present epoch, or present period, the slogan of the independence of Poland.

ENGELS' LETTER TO KAUTSKY

In his pamphlet *Socialism and Colonial Politics* (Berlin, 1907) Kautsky, who was then still a Marxist, published a letter written to him by Engels, dated September 12, 1882, which is extremely interesting in relation to the question under discussion. Here is the principal part of that letter.

". . . In my opinion the colonies proper, *i.e.,* the countries occupied by a European population, Canada, the Cape, Australia, will all become independent; on the other hand the countries inhabited by a native population, which are simply subjugated, India, Algiers, the Dutch, Portuguese, and Spanish possessions, must be taken over for the time being by the proletariat and led as rapidly as possible towards independence. How this process will develop is difficult to say. India will perhaps, indeed very probably, produce a revolution, and as the proletariat emancipating itself cannot conduct any colonial wars, this would have to be given full scope; it would not pass off without all sorts of destruction, of course, but that sort of thing is inseparable from all revolutions. The same might also take place elsewhere, e.g., in Algiers and Egypt, and would certainly be the best thing for us. We shall have enough to do at home. Once Europe is reorganized, and North America, that will furnish such colossal power and such an example that the semi-civilized countries will follow in their wake of their own accord. Economic needs alone will be responsible for this. But as to what social and political phases these countries will then have to pass through before they likewise arrive at socialist organisation, we today can only advance rather idle hypotheses, I think. One thing alone is certain: the victorious proletariat can force no blessings of any kind upon any foreign nation without undermining its own victory by so doing. Which, of course, by no means excludes defensive wars of various kinds. . . ." [26]

Engels by no means supposes that "economics" will of itself and directly remove all difficulties. An economic revolution will be a stimulus to *all* peoples to *tend* towards socialism; but at the same time revolutions—against the socialist state—and wars are possible. Politics will inevitably adapt itself to economics, but not immediately and smoothly, not simply, not directly. Engels mentions as "certain" only one, absolutely internationalist, principle, which he applies to *all* "other nations," *i.e.*, not to colonial nations only, namely: to force blessings upon them would mean undermining the victory of the proletariat.

The proletariat will not become holy and immune from errors and weaknesses merely by virtue of the fact that it has carried out the social revolution. But possible errors (and selfish interest—attempts to ride on the backs of others) will inevitably cause it to appreciate this truth.

We Left Zimmerwaldists are all convinced of what Kautsky, for example, was convinced of before his desertion in 1914 from Marxism to the defense of chauvinism, namely, that the socialist revolu-

114

tion is quite possible in the *very near* future—"any day," as Kautsky himself once put it. National antipathies will not disappear so quickly: the hatred—and perfectly legitimate hatred—of an oppressed nation for its oppressor will *continue* for a while; it will evaporate only *after* the victory of socialism and *after* the final establishment of completely democratic relations between nations. If we desire to be faithful to socialism we must educate the masses in internationalism now, which is impossible in oppressing nations without preaching freedom of secession for oppressed nations.

THE IRISH REBELLION OF 1916

Our theses were written before this rebellion broke out, but it must serve as material for testing our theoretical views.

The views of the opponents of self-determination lead to the conclusion that the vitality of small nations oppressed by imperialism has already been sapped, that they cannot play any role against imperialism, that support of their purely national strivings will lead to nothing, etc. The imperialist war of 1914-16 has provided *facts* which refute such conclusions.

The war proved to be an epoch of crisis for the West European nations, for imperialism as a whole. Every crisis casts off the conventional, it tears away outer wrappings, sweeps away the obsolete and reveals the deeper springs and forces. What has it revealed from the standpoint of the movement of oppressed nations? In the colonies there has been a series of attempts at rebellion, which of course the oppressing nations did all they could to hide from the world by means of the military censorship. Nevertheless, it is known that in Singapore the English brutally suppressed a mutiny among their Indian troops; that there were attempts at rebellion in French Annam (see *Nashe Slovo*) and in the German Cameroons (see Junius' pamphlet), that in Europe, on the one hand, there was a rebellion in Ireland, which the "freedom-loving" English, who did not dare to extend conscription to Ireland, suppressed by executions; and, on the other, the Austrian government sentenced to death the deputies of the Czech Diet "for treason," and shot whole Czech regiments for the same "crime."

This list is far from complete, of course. Nevertheless, it proves that, *owing* to the crisis of imperialism, the flames of national revolt burst out in the colonies *and* in Europe, that national sympathies and antipathies have manifested themselves in spite of draconic threats and measures of repression. And yet the crisis of imperialism has far from reached the highest point of its development: the power of the imperialist bourgeoisie has not yet been undermined (a war of "exhaustion" may bring that about, but it has not been brought about yet); the proletarian movements in the imperialist countries are still very feeble. What will happen when the war has caused complete exhaustion, or when, in at least one state, the power of the bourgeoisie is shaken under the blows of proletarian struggle, as was the power of tsarism in 1905?

In the *Berner Tagwacht,* the organ of the Zimmerwaldists, including some of the Lefts, an article on the Irish Rebellion appeared in the issue of May 9, 1916, entitled "A Played Out Song" and signed with the initials K. R. In this article the Irish Rebellion was declared to be nothing more nor less than a "putsch," for, the author argues, "the Irish question was an agrarian question," the peasants had been appeased by reforms, and the nationalist movement remained only as a *"purely urban petty-bourgeois movement* which, notwithstanding the sensation it caused, had not much social backing."

It is not surprising that this monstrously doctrinaire and pedantic appraisal of the rebellion coincides with the appraisal by a Russian national-liberal Cadet, Mr. A. Kulisher (*Ryech,* No. 102, April 28 [15], 1916), who also dubbed the rebellion "the Dublin putsch."

It is to be hoped that, in accordance with the adage, "it's an ill wind that blows nobody any good," many who fail to realize the morass they are sinking into by repudiating "self-determination," and by treating the national movements of small nations with disdain, will have their eyes opened by the fact that the opinion of a representative of the imperialist bourgeoisie and that of a Social-Democrat "accidentally" coincides.

The term "putsch," in the scientific sense of the word, may be employed only when the attempt at insurrection has revealed nothing but a circle of conspirators or stupid maniacs, and has aroused no sympathy among the masses. The century-old Irish national movement, having passed through various stages and combinations of class interests, expressed itself, *inter alia,* in a mass Irish National Congress in America (*Vorwärts,* March 20, 1916), which passed a resolution calling for Irish independence—it expressed itself in street fighting conducted by a section of the urban petty bourgeoisie and a *section of the workers* after a long period of mass agitation, demonstrations, suppression of papers, etc. Whoever calls *such* an uprising a "putsch" is either a hardened reactionary, or a doctrinaire hope-

116

lessly incapable of picturing to himself a social revolution as a living phenomenon.

To imagine that social revolution is *conceivable* without revolts by small nations in the colonies and in Europe, without the revolutionary outbursts of a section of the petty bourgeoisie *with all its prejudices,* without the movement of non-class conscious proletarian and semi-proletarian masses against the oppression of the landlords, the church, the monarchy, the foreign nations, etc.—to imagine this means *repudiating social revolution.* Only those who imagine that in one place an army will line up and say, "we are for socialism," and in another place another army will say, "we are for imperialism," and that this will be the social revolution, only those who hold such a ridiculously pedantic opinion could vilify the Irish Rebellion by calling it a "putsch."

Whoever expects a "pure" social revolution will *never* live to see it. Such a person pays lip service to revolution without understanding what revolution is.

The Russian Revolution of 1905 was a bourgeois-democratic revolution. It consisted of a series of battles in which *all* the discontented classes, groups, and elements of the population participated. Among these there were masses imbued with the crudest prejudices, with the vaguest and most fantastic aims of struggle; there were small groups which accepted Japanese money, there were speculators and adventurers, etc. *Objectively,* the mass movement broke the back of tsarism and paved the way for democracy; for that reason the class conscious workers led it.

The socialist revolution in Europe *cannot be anything else* than an outburst of mass struggle on the part of all oppressed and discontented elements. Sections of the petty bourgeoisie and of the backward workers will inevitably participate in it—without such participation, *mass* struggle is *impossible,* without it *no* revolution is possible—and just as inevitably will they bring into the movement their prejudices, their reactionary fantasies, their weaknesses and errors. But *objectively* they will attack *capital,* and the class conscious vanguard of the revolution, the advanced proletariat, expressing this objective truth of a heterogeneous and discordant, motley and outwardly incohesive, mass struggle, will be able to unite and direct it, to capture power, to seize the banks, to expropriate the trusts (hated by all, though for different reasons) and introduce other dictatorial measures which in their totality will amount to the overthrow of the bourgeoisie and the victory of socialism, which, however, will by no means immediately "purge" itself of petty-bourgeois slag.

117

Social-Democracy, we read in the Polish theses (I, 4), "must utilize the struggle of the young colonial bourgeoisie against European imperialism *in order to sharpen the revolutionary crisis in Europe.*" (Author's italics.)

Is it not clear that it is least of all permissible to contrast Europe with the colonies in *this* respect? The struggle of the oppressed nations *in Europe,* a struggle capable of going to the lengths of insurrection and street fighting, of breaking down the iron discipline in the army and martial law, will "sharpen the revolutionary crisis in Europe" infinitely more than a much more developed rebellion in a remote colony. A blow delivered against the English imperialist bourgeoisie by a rebellion in Ireland is a hundred times more significant politically than a blow of equal weight delivered in Asia or in Africa.

The French chauvinist press recently reported that the eightieth issue of an illegal newspaper, *Free Belgium,* had appeared in Belgium. Of course, the chauvinist press of France very often tells lies, but this piece of news resembles the truth. While the chauvinist and Kautskyan German Social-Democracy refrained from establishing a free press for itself during the two years of war, and has servilely borne the yoke of military censorship (only the Left radical elements, to their honor be it said, published pamphlets and manifestoes, in spite of the censorship)—an oppressed, civilized nation replied to a military oppression unparalleled in its ferocity, by establishing an organ of revolutionary protest! The dialectics of history is such that small nations, powerless as an *independent* factor in the struggle against imperialism, play a part as one of the ferments, one of the bacilli, which help the *real* power against imperialism to come on the scene, namely, the socialist proletariat.

The General Staffs in the present war assiduously strive to utilize all national and revolutionary movements in the camp of their enemy: the Germans utilize the Irish Rebellion, the French—the Czech movement, etc. From their standpoint they are acting quite properly. A serious war would not be treated seriously if advantage were not taken of the slightest weakness of the enemy, if every opportunity that presented itself were not seized, the more so since it is impossible to know beforehand at what moment, where, and with what force a powder magazine will "explode." We would be very poor revolutionaries if, in the great proletarian war for emancipation and socialism, we did not know how to utilize *every* popular movement against *each separate* disaster caused by imperialism in order to sharpen and extend the crisis. If, on the one hand, we were to declare and to repeat in a thousand keys that we are "opposed" to all national oppression and, on the other hand, we were to describe the heroic revolt of the most mobile and intelligent section of certain classes in an oppressed nation against its oppressors as a "putsch," we would be sinking to the stupid level of the Kautskyists.

The misfortune of the Irish is that they rose prematurely, when the European revolt of the proletariat had *not yet* matured. Capitalism is not so harmoniously built that the various springs of rebellion can immediately merge of their own accord, without reverses and defeats. On the other hand, the very fact that revolts break out at different times, in different places, and are of different kinds, guarantees wide scope and depth to the general movement; only in premature, partial, sporadic, and therefore unsuccessful, revolutionary movements will the masses gain experience, acquire knowledge, gather strength, get to know their real leaders, the socialist proletarians, and in this way prepare for the general onslaught, in the same way as separate strikes, demonstrations, local and national, mutinies in the army, outbreaks among the peasantry, etc., prepared the way for the general onslaught in 1905.

CONCLUSION

Notwithstanding the mistaken assertion of the Polish Social-Democrats, the demand for self-determination of nations has played no less a part in our party propaganda than, for instance, the demand for the armed nation, the separation of the church from the state, election of officers by the people, and other points called "utopian" by philistines. Indeed, the revival of national movements after 1905 naturally stimulated the revival of our agitation; the series of articles published in 1912-13, our party's resolution of 1913, which gave an exact and "anti-Kautskyist" (*i.e.,* irreconcilably hostile to purely verbal "recognition") definition of the *essence* of the question.[27]

Already at that time a fact came to light which cannot be ignored: the opportunists of various nations, the Ukrainian Yurkevich, the Bundist Liebman, and Semkovsky — the Russian henchman of Potresov and Co.—*supported* Rosa Luxemburg's arguments *against* self-determination! Uttered by this Polish Social-Democrat, this was only an incorrect theoretical generalization of the *particular* conditions of the movement in Poland; but on a wider field, not in the conditions of a small state, but on an international field, this at once turned out to be, *objectively,* opportunist support of Great Russian imperialism. The history of the *trends* of political thought (as distinct from personal opinions) has proved the correctness of our program.

And now avowed social-imperialists like Lensch openly oppose both self-determination and the repudiation of annexations. The Kautskyists hypocritically recognise self-determination—in Russia this is the road taken by Trotsky and Martov. In words, *both* declare that they are in favor of self-determination, as Kautsky does. But in practice? Trotsky engages in his customary eclecticism—see his article "Nation and Economics" in *Nashe Slovo*—on the one hand, he says, economics unite nations; on the other hand, national oppression disunites them. What conclusion is to be drawn from this? The conclusion that the prevailing hypocrisy remains unexposed; agitation is lifeless, it fails to touch the main, the fundamental, the material thing that is closest to practice, namely, the attitude to be adopted towards the nation that is oppressed by "my" nation. Martov and the other foreign secretaries preferred simply to forget —convenient forgetfulness!—the fight their colleague and fellow member, Semkovsky, is waging against self-determination. In the Gvozdevist legal press (*Nash Golos*) Martov wrote in *favor* of self-determination and proved the incontrovertible truth that in an imperialist war this does not impose the duty of participating, etc.; but he evaded the main thing—which he evades also in the illegal press!—namely, that *even in peace time* Russia beat the world record of national oppression on the basis of a much more brutal, mediæval, economically backward, military and bureaucratic imperialism. A Russian Social-Democrat who "recognizes" self-determination of nations approximately in the same way as it is recognized by Messrs. Plekhanov, Potresov and Co., *i.e.,* without fighting for freedom of secession for the nations oppressed by tsarism, is *really* an imperialist and a lackey of tsarism.

Whatever the subjective "well-meaning" intentions of Trotsky and Martov may be, they, by their evasions, objectively support Russian social-imperialism. The imperialist epoch has transformed all the "Great" Powers into oppressors of a number of nations, and the development of imperialism will inevitably lead to a clearer division of trends on this question also in international Social-Democracy.

Written in the autumn of 1916.

Collected Works, Vol. XIX, pp. 267-305.

The National Question *

Ever since 1903, when our party adopted its program, we have been encountering the desperate opposition of the Poles. A study of the minutes of the Second Congress reveals that even then the Poles advanced the same argument that they are advancing now, and that the Polish Social-Democrats left the congress because our recognition of the right of nations to self-determination was unacceptable to them. And we have been confronted with this question ever since. Though imperialism was already in existence in 1903, no mention was made of it in the arguments that were then advanced. Both then and now the position of Polish Social-Democracy is a strange and monstrous error. These people wish to reduce the position of our party to that of the chauvinists.

Owing to Russia's age-long oppression of Poland the policy of Poland is thoroughly nationalistic, and the entire Polish people are thoroughly imbued with but one idea—revenge on the Muscovites. No one has oppressed the Poles so much as have the Russian people. In the hands of the tsars the Russian people have served as the executioner of Polish freedom. No one dislikes Russia so intensely as do the Poles, and this has brought about a peculiar situation. Owing to the Polish bourgeoisie, Poland has become an obstacle in the path of the socialist movement. Let the whole world burn, as long as Poland is free. Of course, to put the question in this way is to mock at internationalism. Of course, violence now reigns in Poland, but for the Polish nationalists to count on Russia liberating Poland is treason to the International. The Polish nationalists have so imbued the Polish people with their spirit, however, that this view prevails.

The great historical merit of our comrades, the Polish Social-Democrats, is that they have advanced the slogan of internation-

* At the Bolshevik (April) Conference, held April 29 (May 12), 1917, soon after Lenin's return to Russia, Stalin made the report on the National Question, presented the resolution and summarized the discussion.[28] Lenin made this speech as a contribution to that discussion.—*Ed.*

alism, that they have said: we treasure the fraternal alliance of the proletariat of all countries more than anything else and we shall never go to war for the liberation of Poland. This is their great merit, and this is why we have always regarded only these Social-Democratic comrades in Poland as Socialists. The others are patriots, Polish Plekhanovs. But this unique situation, in which, in order to safeguard socialism, it was found necessary to fight against rabid, morbid nationalism, has been productive of a strange phenomenon: comrades come to us and say that we must renounce the freedom of Poland, its right to secession.

Why should we, Great Russians, who have been oppressing a greater number of nations than any other people, why should we repudiate the right of secession for Poland, the Ukraine, Finland? We are asked to become chauvinists, because by doing so we would ease the position of the Social-Democrats in Poland. We do not claim the liberation of Poland because the Polish people dwell between two states which are capable of fighting—they say. But instead of saying that the Polish workers should argue in this way, *viz.,* only those Social-Democrats remain democrats who consider that the Polish people ought to be free, for there is no place for chauvinists in the ranks of the Socialist Party—the Polish Social-Democrats argue that precisely because they find the union with the Russian workers advantageous, they are opposed to Poland's secession. They have a perfect right to do so. But these people do not wish to understand that in order to strengthen internationalism there is no need to reiterate the same words; what we in Russia do is to stress the right of secession for the subject nations, while in Poland we must stress the right of such nations to unite. The right to unite implies the right to secede. We Russians must emphasize the right to secede, while the Poles must emphasize the right to unite.

We notice here a number of sophisms leading to the complete renunciation of Marxism. Comrade Pyatakov's standpoint is a repetition of Rosa Luxemburg's standpoint. . . .* (Holland is an example.) This is how Comrade Pyatakov argues, and this is also how he confutes himself. Theoretically he is opposed to the right of secession, but to the people he declares that he who is opposed to the right of secession is no Socialist. What Comrade Pyatakov said here was evidence of incredible confusion. In Western Europe most of the countries settled their national question long ago. When people say that the national question has been settled, they

* An omission in the minutes.—*Ed.*

122

mean Western Europe. Comrade Pyatakov applies this where it does not belong, to Eastern Europe, and we find ourselves in a ridiculous position.

Think of the terrible mess that results! Finland is right at our side. Comrade Pyatakov gives no definite answer as to Finland; he is in utter confusion. In yesterday's *Rabochaya Gazeta* we read that separatism is growing in Finland. Finns arriving here inform us that separatism is maturing in their country, because the Cadets have refused to grant it complete autonomy. There, a crisis is maturing; dissatisfaction with Governor-General Rodichev is rife, but *Robochaya Gazeta* insists that the Finns ought to wait for the constituent assembly, that then an agreement will be concluded between Finland and Russia. An agreement; what about? There Finns must maintain that they are entitled to determine their own destiny in their own way, and any Great Russian who denies this right is a chauvinist. It would be another thing entirely if we said to the Finnish worker: decide as you think fit. . . .*

Comrade Pyatakov simply rejects our slogan when he says that this means giving no slogan for the socialist revolution, but he himself has not offered any slogan. The method of accomplishing a socialist revolution under the slogan, "down with frontiers," is utterly absurd. We were not able to publish the article in which I described this view as "imperialist economism." [29] What does the "method" of socialist revolution under the slogan, "down with frontiers," mean? We maintain that the state is necessary, and the existence of a state presupposes frontiers. The state may, of course, be ruled by a bourgeois government, while we want Soviets. But even Soviets are confronted with the question of frontiers. What does "down with frontiers" mean? This is the beginning of anarchy. . . . The "method" of socialist revolution under the slogan, "down with frontiers," is a hodge-podge. When the time is ripe for a socialist revolution, when the revolution finally occurs, it will sweep across into other countries, and we shall help it to do so, but how, we do not know. "The method of socialist revolution" is a mere phrase, devoid of content. In so far as the bourgeois revolution has left some problems unsolved, we stand for their solution. As regards the separatist movement, we are indifferent, neutral. If Finland, if Poland, if the Ukraine break away from Russia, there is nothing bad about that. What is there bad about it?

* An omission in the minutes.—*Ed.*

Anyone who says there is, is a chauvinist. It would be madness to continue the policy of Tsar Nicholas. Norway separated from Sweden. . . . Once upon a time Alexander I and Napoleon traded peoples, once upon a time tsars traded portions of Poland. Are we to continue these tactics of the tsars? This is the repudiation of the tactics of internationalism, this is chauvinism of the worst brand. Suppose Finland does secede, what is there bad about that? Among both peoples, among the proletariat of Norway and that of Sweden, mutual confidence increased after separation. The Swedish land-lords wanted to wage war, but the Swedish workers resisted this and said: we shall not go to such a war.

All that the Finns want now is autonomy. We stand for giving Finland complete liberty; that will increase their confidence in Russian democracy, and when they are given the right to secede they will not do so. While Mr. Rodichev goes to Finland to haggle over autonomy, our Finnish comrades come here and say: we must have autonomy. But fire is opened on them from the whole battery and they are told: "Wait for the constituent assembly." We, however, say: "Any Russian Socialist who denies freedom to Finland is a chauvinist."

We say that frontiers are determined by the will of the popula-tion. Russia, don't dare fight over Courland! Germany, withdraw your armies from Courland! This is our solution of the problem of secession. The proletariat cannot resort to violence, for it must not interfere with the freedom of peoples. The slogan, "down with frontiers," will become a true slogan only when the socialist rev-olution has become a reality, and not a method. Then we shall say: comrades, come to us. . . .

Now war is an entirely different matter. When necessary, we shall not refuse to wage a revolutionary war. We are not paci-fists. . . . But while we have Milyukov, and while he sends Rod-ichev to Finland, where he shamefully haggles with the Finnish people, we say to the Russian people: don't dare rape Finland; no nation can be free if it oppresses other nations. In our resolu-tion concerning Borgbjerg,* we state: withdraw your armies, and

* By this resolution the conference rejected the invitation of the Danish Social-Democrat, Borgbjerg, to take part in an international "congress of Socialists for the purpose of supporting peace," which the German social-chau-vinists, acting on the instructions of the German bourgeoisie and of the Ger-man government, proposed to call "on the condition that Germany abandon most of her annexations." The French and English social-chauvinists refused to take part in this congress, they in turn were acting on the instructions of their respective bourgeoisie and governments. The Russian Mensheviks

let the nation settle this question itself. But if the Soviet seizes power tomorrow, it will no longer be a "method of socialist revolution"; we shall then say: Germany, withdraw your armies from Poland; Russia, withdraw your armies from Armenia—otherwise, the whole thing will be a deception.

Regarding his oppressed Poland, Comrade Dzerzhinsky* tells us that everybody is a chauvinist there. But why does not any Pole tell us what we ought to do with Finland, what we ought to do with the Ukraine? We have been arguing about this question so much, ever since 1903, that it is difficult to say much about it now. Go where you please. . . . He who does not accept this point of view is an annexationist, a chauvinist. We are for the fraternal union of all nations. If there is a Ukrainian republic and a Russian republic, there will be closer contact, greater confidence between the two. If the Ukrainians see that we have a Soviet republic, they will not break away. But if we retain the Milyukov republic, they will break away. When Comrade Pyatakov, contradicting his own views, said that he is opposed to the forcible retention of nations within the frontiers, he really admitted the principle of self-determination. We do not in the least want the peasant in Khiva to live under the Khan of Khiva. By developing our revolution we shall influence the oppressed masses. Agitation among the oppressed masses should be carried on only in this manner.

But any Russian Socialist who does not recognise the freedom of Finland and the Ukraine is bound to degenerate into a chauvinist. And no sophisms, no references to his own "method" will help him to justify himself.

Speech at the All-Russian April Conference of the Russian Social-Democratic Labor Party, April 29 (May 12), 1917.

Collected Works, Vol. XX, Book I, pp. 310-14.

and Socialist-Revolutionaries accepted Borgbjerg's invitation. The resolution adopted at the Bolshevik Conference on this question was proposed by Lenin, who in his speech said: ". . . back of this whole comedy of an alleged Socialist congress there is a very real political maneuver of German imperialism. The German capitalists use the German social-chauvinists for the purpose of inviting the social-chauvinists of all countries to the conference. That is why it is necessary to launch a great campaign."—*Ed.*

* Felix Dzerzhinsky, well-known Bolshevik of Polish descent. After the October Revolution held several ministerial posts until his death in 1926.—*Ed.*

REFERENCE NOTES

1. See Karl Marx, *Capital*, Vol. I, p. 790, *note*, New York, 1947

2. *The Correspondence of Karl Marx and Frederick Engels,* p. 37, New York, 1934

3. *Ibid.,* p. 162

4. *Ibid.,* pp. 207-08

5. For part of letter, see *Ibid.,* p. 228

6. *Ibid.,* p. 229

7. For part of letter, see *Ibid.,* p. 264

8. *Ibid.,* p. 263

9. *Ibid.,* p. 265

10. *Ibid.,* pp. 280-81

11. See letter to Engels, June 7, 1866, *Correspondence Between Karl Marx and Frederick Engels,* Vol. III, p. 323, Stuttgart, 1921, German ed.

12. See letter to Engels, June 20, 1866, *The Selected Correspondence of Karl Marx and Frederick Engels,* p. 208, New York, 1942

13. See letter to Engels, November 2, 1867, *Ibid.,* p. 228

14. See Karl Marx, *Letters to Kugelmann,* pp. 95-96, New York, 1934

15. See V. I. Lenin, *Collected Works,* Vol. XVII, pp. 11-13, Russian ed.

16. See pp. 73-85 of present volume

17. See p. 74 of present volume

18. Karl Marx, *Critique of the Gotha Programme,* p. 18, New York, 1938

19. See pp. 79-80 of present volume

20. See pp. 81-82 of present volume

21. See pp. 77-78 of present volume

22. See V. I. Lenin, *Collected Works,* Vol. XVIII, pp. 76-83, 145-50, New York, 1930

23. See pp. 77-78, 80-81 of present volume

24. See V. I. Lenin, *Collected Works,* Vol. XIX, pp. 199-213, New York, 1942

25. See pp. 80-81 of present volume

26. *The Correspondence of Karl Marx and Frederick Engels,* p. 399

27. V. I. Lenin, *Collected Works,* Vol. XVII, pp. 11-13, Russian ed.

28. See Joseph Stalin, *Marxism and the National Question,* pp. 69-75, New York, 1942

29. See V. I. Lenin, "A Caricature of Marxism and 'Imperialist Economism,'" *Collected Works,* Vol. XIX, pp. 214-63